Why Your Students Do What They Do and What to Do When They Do It

A Practical Guide for Understanding Classroom Behavior

GRADES 6-12

Roger Pierangelo & George A. Giuliani

Research Press ● 2612 North Mattis Avenue ● Champaign, Illinois 61822
(800) 519-2707 ● www.researchpress.com

Cover design by Linda Brown, Positive ID Graphic Design, Inc.
Composition by Jeff Helgesen
Printed by McNaughton & Gunn

ISBN 0–87822–455–6
Library of Congress Catalog Number 00–106529

To my loving wife, Jackie; my two beautiful children, Jacqueline and Scott; and my parents, who got so much pleasure from being parents

To my sister, Carole, who would make any brother proud, and my brother-in-law, Dr. George Giuliani, who throughout our relationship has always been there unconditionally

To the memory of Rochelle Crane, who always symbolized the word courage *and whose greatness lives on in the hearts of all who knew her*

—R. P.

To my wife, Anita, and my two children, Collin and Brittany, who give me the greatest life imaginable

To my parents, George and Carol Giuliani, who always made going to school a rewarding experience by giving me the self-confidence to believe I could succeed at anything I did

—G. A. G.

Contents

Common Classroom Problems and Concerns

Preface

All teachers face a variety of personality types, issues, and challenges in the classroom. However, few have had the opportunity to take the courses on human psychology and interpersonal dynamics that would help them appreciate the nature or meaning of students' symptomatic behavior. For the most part, teachers are put on the firing line with little or no training in why adolescents do what they do. They are expected to help children learn but are not trained in understanding the underlying psychological causes that may be at work in adolescents' interpersonal and academic difficulties. This lack of understanding can be very frustrating for teachers and students alike, and it hinders progress toward students' academic success. All teachers need to understand the inner workings of adolescents who are experiencing trouble in school. Understanding what causes adolescents to choose certain behavioral patterns can help teachers reach these students sooner as well as prevent long-lasting scars.

Why Your Students Do What They Do is a unique guide, designed to help all middle- and high-school teachers understand why their students do what they do and what to do when they do it. This book offers insight into the inner dynamics, conflicts, fears, symptoms, and tensions of students who may be experiencing difficulty learning or behaving in the classroom. It is a must-have reference for anyone involved in the process of teaching adolescents at these levels. It can help teachers, parents, administrators, and other school personnel toward a greater understanding of issues pertaining to the psychology of children in the classroom.

This book focuses on the kinds of behavioral and learning problems teachers observe on a daily basis—everything from unexcused absences to clowning, from impulsivity to test failure. These common classroom concerns are organized by topic, with each topic including a description of possible causes for the difficulty and practical suggestions for intervention. For easy access, the topics are presented in alphabetical order according to main word. A quick perusal of the table of contents will guide readers to topics of interest—for example, *unexcused absences* is listed in the contents under *absences, unexcused.* Similarly, *short attention span* is listed under *attention span, short.*

We have organized the description of possible causes for each classroom problem or concern according to eight general categories: academic, environmental, intellectual, linguistic, medical, perceptual, psychological, and social. Readers will note that not all categories are represented for all topics. A category is included if in our opinion the factors associated with it commonly pertain to the problem. If factors in a given category are not frequently associated with the problem, we have omitted that category. Our omission of a category does not mean that associated factors could not play a part in any given classroom situation—indeed they may— only that in our experience other categories include more likely causes. Following the discussion of possible reasons students may exhibit a given behavior, we describe a number of possible responses educators might choose to make. These practical suggestions should be viewed as guidelines only; the details of the individual situation will of course dictate the best responses in any given case.

We view this book as a basic reference tool to help educators identify classroom problems early on and begin to understand the depth of the issues that may be involved. Insight into underlying psychological causes can help teachers work more effectively on the real issues that may be creating problems both inside and outside of school. In addition, competence in this area can help teachers foster confidence and respect in students and parents. We hope that if you have taken up this book you will find the information it presents to be helpful. We also hope that you will be encouraged to continue your study in this complex subject.

Acknowledgments

I would like to thank the St. Joseph's College grant committee for their financial and emotional support for my work on this book. Their continued encouragement is much appreciated. I am also grateful to St. Joseph's College itself, the greatest institution at which a person could teach. They truly live their motto, *esse non videri*, to be and not to seem. I wish to express my special appreciation to my colleagues in the Psychology Department. It is a true pleasure to be part of such a wonderful team. I have the greatest respect for the efficiency, dedication, and organizational abilities of Erin Bailey, my research assistant, whose hard work locating information was essential in making this book a reality.

—G. A. G.

Introduction

Adolescents and adults are exposed to a variety of stressors almost every day. All stressors create tension, tension that must be relieved either verbally or behaviorally. If an adolescent is unable to communicate his or her feelings, as is the case for many, then that tension will exhibit itself in symptomatic behavior. This symptomatic behavior is what teachers see every day in the classroom: One student constantly seeks the teacher's attention. Another procrastinates until it is too late to complete assignments. Yet others defy authority, talk excessively, or can't seem to handle criticism. Although such symptoms may not always indicate a serious problem, if they are frequent, intense, and long-lasting, they certainly warrant attention.

Teachers are confronted with symptomatic behavior every day. If they do not understand the nature of a symptom, they will be likely to treat the symptoms as the problem. Treating a fever as a problem will never cure the infection. Although it is true that teachers need not "cure" the problem, it is important that they recognize symptom patterns of a more serious condition so that proper referrals can be made and more serious problems averted.

WHY STUDENTS MAY EXHIBIT PROBLEM BEHAVIORS

There may be any number of causes for an adolescent's symptomatic behavior—or multiple causes may be in effect. However, to structure the discussion of common classroom problems and concerns presented in the book's main section, we can pinpoint eight general areas in which difficulties can arise:

1. Academic
2. Environmental
3. Intellectual
4. Linguistic
5. Medical
6. Perceptual
7. Psychological
8. Social

Factors in any of these areas, if intense enough, can create class-room symptoms resulting in academic, behavioral, or social dysfunction. It is important to point out that a great deal of overlap exists among these categories and that, conversely, not all of these categories are pertinent to every classroom difficulty. If in the discussion of a classroom concern a category is not represented, it means that factors associated with that category are not generally applicable to the problem and that we have chosen to focus on more likely origins of the difficulty.

Academic Factors

It seems obvious that, at times, academic deficits may impair an adolescent's ability to function in the classroom. Factors that can contribute to academic dysfunction include but are not limited to the following:

- Developmental reading disorders
- Developmental math disorders
- Developmental writing disorders
- Developmental spelling disorders
- Poor prior teaching
- Lack of basic skills
- Inconsistency during critical periods of skill development
- Problems in concept formation
- Lack of reinforcement

Underachievement due to academic factors in spite of adequate intelligence is very frustrating to students, teachers, and parents. Many times, these problems can be resolved with extra help, tutors, reinforcement, and so on. However, if academic problems are unidentified for a long period of time, then secondary (i.e., psychological) factors will begin to develop as well. Whatever the exact nature of the difficulty, academic factors need to be addressed as quickly as possible so the student does not become blocked at a critical stage of skill development.

Environmental Factors

Environmental factors are factors the adolescent may be exposed to at home or in the community that may have a profound impact on the adolescent's ability to function in school. These factors may include home issues such as the following:

- Parental abuse
- Parental fighting
- Separation and/or divorce
- Family illness
- Economic hardship
- Loss of parent's job
- Moving into a new neighborhood
- Serious sibling rivalry
- Family mental illness
- Relatives residing in the home
- Alcoholism
- Drug abuse

Environmental factors may also concern community issues such as these, among others:

- Problems with neighbors
- Poor reputation in the neighborhood
- Isolation of the family from neighbors
- Problems with the law

Whether originating at home or in the community, environmental factors tend to add a great deal of stress to an adolescent's life, stress that may manifest itself in symptoms at school. One needs to be aware of the possibility that classroom symptoms resulting in dysfunction may actually have their roots in these types of issues outside of school.

Intellectual Factors

Sometimes an adolescent's difficulties in school may be the result of intellectual factors. When these factors are present, the student's stress may be manifested in a variety of symptoms. This category includes undetected limited intellectual ability and undetected gifted intellectual capacity.

Limited intellectual ability can cause a great deal of stress in an adolescent, resulting from fear of social ridicule, teachers' or parents' negative reactions or disappointment, and so on. This problem may not always be detected early. Some teachers may misinterpret this factor as immaturity, stubbornness, or lack of motivation. When limited intellectual ability is not quickly identified, the student deals with the stress of the situation through many symptoms (e.g., avoidance, procrastination). These symptom patterns may not be fully understood by teachers, who may try to remove the symptoms, believing they are the real problem. If this occurs, because the problem still exists and will continue to create tension, alternative symptoms will eventually arise.

Undetected gifted intellectual capacity can be equally stressful. Gifted adolescents may become bored in class and get into trouble as a result of lack of direction and stimulation. A gifted mind needs stimulation in order to run properly. Teachers may not detect giftedness for several reasons. First, if they are focusing on the student's negative symptoms, they may consider him or her a behavior problem. In their minds, giftedness and behavioral problems do not exist at the same time. Second, some teachers may feel inadequate to deal with such an intellectually capable student. If the student knows more than they do, they may sense the potential for an ego-deflating situation.

In either case, intellectual factors need to be identified early. Understanding the symptom patterns that may identify these problems will help these students succeed in school.

Linguistic Factors

Language provides the foundation upon which communication, problem solving, integrating, analyzing, and synthesizing of knowledge take place. Therefore, deficits in language can have a profound impact on the ability of an individual to learn and function competently and confidently in interaction with the world. They may result in difficulties expressed in the following areas, among others:

- Nonverbal language
- Oral language (i.e., listening and speaking)
- Written language (i.e., reading and writing)
- Pragmatic language (e.g., using language for a specific purpose, such as asking for help)
- Phonology

- Audiology
- Word retrieval
- Articulation

It is clear how important language processing can be to a student's successful school adaptation. The adolescent may not acquire critical knowledge, may connect incorrect bits of information in memory, and may have ineffective means of showing others all that he or she knows. How quickly a person can access words or ideas in memory further influences his or her use of language. A student who must struggle to find an appropriate term is at a great disadvantage in a learning and social environment. As he or she grapples to retrieve a word, others have moved on. Such problems can result in lowered levels of achievement and in feelings of confusion, helplessness, and frustration. Language factors are also commonly expressed when the language of instruction is not the student's first language. When students must learn English at the same time they must master content and keep up with peers, they are at risk for learning problems and resulting symptomatology.

Before embarking on an extensive (and expensive) battery of tests, examiners should ensure that any apparent speech or language impairment is not actually the result of a medical problem. A hearing impairment may prevent the adolescent from understanding spoken language and learning to use or understand words. Similarly, many adolescents with physical disabilities may not be able to speak clearly enough to be understood but, when provided with assistive technology (e.g., speech synthesizers, computers), may show themselves to be competent users of language.

Medical Factors

Medical factors that may contribute to an adolescent's academic or social dysfunction are numerous. Although teachers are not expected to be doctors, they do need to be aware that certain medical conditions may manifest as symptoms in the classroom. For the most part, teachers may assume that any serious medical condition has already been identified by the adolescent's pediatrician or parent. However, this may not always be true, especially in the case of a younger adolescent.

Medical problems that may impair a student's ability to function adequately in the classroom include but are not limited to the following:

- Attention deficit/hyperactivity disorder (AD/HD)
- Vision problems
- Hearing problems
- Neurological problems
- Muscular problems
- Coordination problems

Medical conditions that may affect academic and social adaptation are too numerous to discuss comprehensively in this book; however, we have attempted to describe the most common medical factors when these contribute to symptomatic behavior in the classroom.

Attention deficit/hyperactivity disorder (AD/HD) is quite common in the classrooms and is associated with many of the symptomatic behaviors described in this book. This disorder is grouped under the medical category because, although its cause is unknown, recent research suggests that it is neurological with a genetic component. If you can confirm that a student has been diagnosed with AD/HD, through school records or discussion with the school psychologist, you will be far better able to help that student. If a student has not received a diagnosis but you suspect the disorder is present, you will likely want to confer with the school's pupil personnel team before discussing your concerns with the parents. The chart on the next page lists the diagnostic criteria for AD/HD. Accurate and early diagnosis is crucial to facilitate development of a treatment plan and reduce the chances that the student will develop secondary problems.

Perceptual Factors

Perception is a process that involves many different areas. While most of us take perceptual abilities for granted, for some adolescents problems in this area contribute to very difficult, frustrating, and deflating experiences.

The learning process is like an assembly line through which information received travels. The information received is filtered through a series of psychological processes. As information pro-

Symptoms of Attention Deficit/Hyperactivity Disorder

INATTENTION (six or more of the following)

Often fails to give close attention to details or makes careless mistakes.

Often has difficulty sustaining attention in tasks or play activities.

Often does not seem to listen when spoken to directly.

Often does not follow through on instructions and fails to finish schoolwork or chores.

Often has difficulty organizing tasks and activities.

Often avoids, dislikes, or is reluctant to engage in tasks that require sustained mental effort (such as schoolwork or homework).

Often loses things necessary for tasks or activities (e.g., toys, school assignments, pencils, books, or tools).

Is often disracted by extraneous stimuli.

Is often forgetful in daily activities.

HYPERACTIVITY-IMPULSIVITY (at least six of the following)

Hyperactivity

Often fidgets with hands or feet or squirms in seat.

Often leaves seat in classroom or in other situations in which remaining seated is expected.

Often runs about or climbs excessively in situations in which remaining seated is expected.

Often runs about or climbs excessively in situations in which it is inappropriate (in adolescents, may be limited to feelings of restlessness).

Often has difficulty playing or engaging in leisure activities quietly.

Is often "on the go" or often acts as if "driven by a motor."

Often talks excessively.

Impulsivity

Often blurts out answers before questions have been completed.

Often has difficulty waiting for a turn.

Often interrupts or intrudes on others (e.g., butts into conversations or games).

To constitute a diagnosis of AD/HD:

Some symptoms must have been present before age 7.

Symptoms cause significant impairment in social, academic, or occupational functioning.

Impairment must be present in two or more settings (e.g., at home and at school).

Note: From *Diagnostic and Statistical Manual of Mental Disorders* (DSM-IV; 4th ed.), 1994, Washington, DC: American Psychiatric Association. Adapted by permission.

gresses, it is given meaning and organized. When we evaluate a student's perceptual abilities, we are attempting to find out whether a deficit in some area of the learning process may be slowing down processing, thereby interfering in the student's ability to receive, organize, memorize, or express information.

Perceptual difficulties can impair a student's ability to function, both academically and socially. Although perceptual deficits are often misunderstood or undiagnosed, they can account for symptomatic behavior in high-risk students. Being able to identify the symptoms that may be caused by serious perceptual deficits can reduce an adolescent's frustration, both in and out of the classroom.

Psychological Factors

Psychological factors that may be contributing to an adolescent's dysfunction in school may include but are not limited to the following:

- Depression
- Anxiety
- Eating disorders
- Personality disorders
- Schizophrenia
- Phobias
- Obsessive-compulsive disorder
- Psychosexual dysfunction
- Substance abuse
- Sleep disorders
- Brief situational disturbances or adjustment reactions
- Separation anxiety
- Oppositional defiant or conduct disorder

Specific psychological problems like these can create an inordinate amount of tension and subsequent behavioral symptoms. In addition, psychological stress in today's society may account for the problems of many adolescents in the classroom. Teachers need to be informed of the ways these problems may manifest themselves so they can make the proper referrals as quickly as possible.

Once a problem is identified, a useful treatment plan can be devised, including the home, the school psychologist or an outside therapist, medication (if necessary), and classroom management techniques to reduce any secondary effects of the symptoms the problem has generated.

Social Factors

Social factors may contribute to an adolescent's stress and consequently interfere with learning. Although social status is a crucial factor at many ages, it is of special concern in young as well as older adolescents. Social pressures and peer influence sometimes create an imbalance in a student's functioning: Because energy is expended to cope with social issues and conflicts, less energy is available for school-related concerns.

Social factors that may lower an adolescent's available energy and result in academic dysfunction include the following, among others:

- Peer rejection
- Preoccupation with boyfriends or girlfriends
- Low social status
- Social victimization (e.g., scapegoating, social intimidation, being the target of bullying behavior)
- Need to control others
- Peer competition
- Social isolation
- Social overindulgence

When adolescents have serious social concerns, their thoughts may be obsessive. The symptoms associated with such concerns can be intense; if the problem is not identified quickly, it can lead to numerous secondary issues.

WHAT TO DO WHEN PROBLEM BEHAVIORS OCCUR

When teachers understand the nature of symptomatic behavior and make proper referrals for guidance, they can help adolescents avoid more serious, long-lasting difficulties. Even if a student's symptomatic behavior has been correctly identified and necessary referrals made, the student's problems may take a while to dissipate. While teachers are waiting to receive guidance or information, as well as during the time the underlying problem is being resolved, they can respond in ways that calm the student, provide suitable boundaries, reduce classroom frustration, and otherwise deal with the situation in a positive way.

The possible responses we describe can help reduce the impact of a troubled adolescent's symptomatic behavior. Often these are commonsense suggestions—discuss the problem with the student, consult with colleagues, confer with parents. Where appropriate, we have suggested responses specific to the topic or described a step-by-step procedure for dealing with the situation. It is critical to understand that patterns of inappropriate behavior—especially if they are severe or persist—should be shared with parents and with other members of the school staff, especially the school social work or counseling staff, the school psychologist, and the pupil personnel team. Collaborating with others will enhance any responses an individual teacher chooses to make.

Unexcused Absences

Why Students
May Exhibit This Behavior

ACADEMIC   Students may miss school because they have not completed their homework or prepared for tests, and they may fear the reaction of the teacher or their peers.

ENVIRONMENTAL   Chronic unexcused absence may indicate problems at home concerning family routines, rules, supervision, authority issues, or boundaries. Family dysfunction can produce a chaotic and unstable environment, which can lead to truancy.

INTELLECTUAL   Students with limited intelligence may miss school because they know that they cannot keep up with their classmates. They struggle every day, trying their hardest, but their below-average capabilities do not let them excel as their classmates do.

LINGUISTIC   Adolescents with language problems or disabilities may miss school out of frustration. Their problems with language become such a source of tension that, eventually, it is no longer enjoyable nor worthwhile to attend school.

MEDICAL   Certain types of medical problems can affect school attendance. However, if a medical condition is the cause for unexcused absences, the parent will need to provide some documentation.

PERCEPTUAL   Adolescents with perceptual problems may miss school out of anxiety and frustration.

PSYCHOLOGICAL   Depression, anxiety, and low self-esteem are just a few of the many possible psychological reasons for unexcused absences. Students with such problems may not see school as being constructive. They have so many underlying issues and such low energy levels that they cannot focus on schoolwork and interact with their peers.

SOCIAL   Some students may skip school to avoid uncomfortable confrontations with peers before, during, or after school. A social argument, bullying, or fear of retaliation can be at the root of an unexcused absence.

What to Do

- Contact the student's parents. They may be unaware of their student's unexcused absences.
- Ask the student why he is missing school. If he has shown a serious pattern of unexcused absences and offers a simple illogical answer, then the truth may lie elsewhere.
- Ask the school psychologist whether there are any external circumstances surrounding this student's absences.
- If it is determined that the student's unexcused absences are due to family issues, consider meeting or having an administrator meet with the parents to discuss the school's concerns.
- If it is determined that the unexcused absences are due to some behavior on the part of the student and persist in spite of parental efforts to get the student to school, try the following techniques:

  1. Give the student a specific responsibility to fulfill first thing in the morning to encourage him to be in school.
  2. Provide consequences for unexcused absences. One effective way of doing this is making the student responsible for the time missed if he does not have an acceptable reason for being absent.
  3. Place the student in a position of leadership for some in-school group activity.
  4. Reward the student for attending school. This does not require a tangible reward but merely verbal praise.

- Consult with the school counseling or social work staff or the school psychologist about the possibility of developing a behavioral contract for the student.
- If the problem persists, consult with the school's pupil personnel team.

Overall Academic Failure

Why Students May Exhibit This Behavior

ACADEMIC   Clearly, a lack of skills can have a direct effect on a student's ability to perform in school. Whether the skills deficiency arises from inconsistent school attendance, frequent changes in school due to family moves, poor teaching, trauma, or other issues, the result is the same. Pure academic deficiencies tend to accumulate year to year if not recognized and addressed early. Eventually, the student experiences so much pressure and feels so far behind that she gives up.

ENVIRONMENTAL   Academic failure may result from a variety of environmental factors. Students from dysfunctional homes may not have experienced the routine, supervision, and boundaries required at certain ages to enhance achievement. Also, students from homes with high levels of tension (e.g., where abuse or alcoholism is present) may be so preoccupied with fear of parental reaction or upsetting a parent that they cannot muster enough energy to concentrate, focus, and retain information during school. Sometimes, students fail because of excessive parental expectations that they feel they cannot fulfill, so they give up. Others may suffer from competition or comparison with more academically successful siblings.

INTELLECTUAL   Intellectual ability is a significant factor in a student's academic performance level. Students with limited intellectual capacity will lag behind other students and may eventually give up. Conversely, gifted students who go unrecognized may find school boring or not challenging and thus be unmotivated to perform.

LINGUISTIC   Students who have language disorders or for whom the language of instruction is not their first language may fail in school because they cannot understand what is being taught and expected of them.

MEDICAL   Some medical conditions may result in limitations in performance (e.g., an eye muscle problem that impairs vision), preoccupation with a health condition (e.g., a heart condition), or direct impediments to performance (e.g., a neurological disorder).

PERCEPTUAL   Perceptual deficits that result in learning disabilities can lead to school failure. Students who have slow processing speeds due to such deficits will lag behind, feel inadequate, and in many cases give up. Processing information slowly, in spite of adequate intelligence, can be very frustrating and embarrassing. Students thus affected may develop academic resistance secondary to the fear of being ridiculed.

PSYCHOLOGICAL   Students may fail in school as a result of low self-esteem, low confidence, high anxiety, or depression. Any of these factors can interfere with a student's ability to perform adequately and consistently over time.

SOCIAL   Some adolescents fail in school because they want to be accepted by social groups that do not respect academic performance. Bright students are sometimes drawn to social groups of underachievers, and the group message is clear: "Don't achieve if you want to be part of this group." The group message is designed to protect the members from realizing their inadequacy. Other students may fail because they do not feel they can compete or keep up with peers' performance.

What to Do

- Review the student's records, including past teacher comments, for similar symptoms exhibited in earlier grades. If precursor behavior is found, the problem may be more serious. If possible, contact the previous teachers for feedback on what they tried, what worked, and what did not work: You do not want to repeat something that proved ineffective in the past.

- Review past report cards for consistent difficulties in certain subject areas. Sometimes students with serious learning problems or learning disabilities show patterns of academic failure over long periods.

- Review the student's group achievement test scores, as they may give you some idea of skill levels. However, be aware that a student with a serious learning problem may not have taken a group-administered test seriously.

- Review the student's IQ scores if they are available. They may offer insight into the student's overall intellectual ability. If you believe the student is working to her capabilities, has an average or better IQ, and yet is still failing in school, the case warrants immediate attention.

- Meet with the school nurse to review the student's medical records for any medical condition that might be contributing to school failure. Ask about hearing and vision and whether or not the student is on any medications.

- Consult with the school counseling or social work staff, the school psychologist, or the pupil personnel team.

High Activity Level

ACADEMIC Students who are failing in school can become very nervous and anxious because they know that they are not doing as well as others. Anxiety over schoolwork can lead to nervous tension, manifested in a high activity level.

ENVIRONMENTAL Some adolescents live in homes where the pace is very rapid. Everyone moves very fast, and this is what they are exposed to day after day. They then copy the behavior modeled at home.

INTELLECTUAL Students with limited intelligence may not understand that there is a time and place for high activity. These students may just constantly be on the move, simply because they do not understand that high activity levels can be inappropriate at certain times.

MEDICAL Students who have attention deficit/hyperactivity disorder (AD/HD) will be prone to experience high activity levels.

PSYCHOLOGICAL When adolescents feel tense and nervous about personal problems, conflicts, fears, and the like, the result can be high activity levels. In other cases, they may exhibit high activity as a means of being in the spotlight and maintaining others' attention.

SOCIAL Some students can be very active because they are anticipating events in school or with their peers. Their hyperactivity is, in actuality, excitement about what is coming up socially. Also, students may exhibit hyperactive behavior as a group because they feed off one another in this behavior. Individually, each student may be fine, but collectively they become a wild bunch.

What to Do

- Because it is almost assured that you will have one or two students with AD/HD in your class every year, it is imperative to expect this behavior to occur and plan ahead. You should plan what to do if a student's hyperactivity affects the class, then enforce your rules if this happens.

- Ask the school psychologist whether the student has been diagnosed with AD/HD and/or has ever received special education services.

- Ask the school nurse whether the student is on any medication for AD/HD (e.g., Ritalin).

- If the foregoing possibilities have been ruled out, speak privately with the student and ask him why he behaves in this manner. Overactivity is often a way of seeking attention. Explain to the student that you recognize what he is doing, and establish some way to show him that you will recognize him whenever he makes a particular gesture or statement.

- Explain the class rules to the student and clarify what is appropriate behavior. It is possible that this student has not experienced the type of structure necessary for his present grade level.

- Contact the parents if the student's behavior is seriously affecting his social, emotional, or academic functioning. However, do not discuss the idea of medication with the parents. Although you may feel that medication is appropriate, this is not your role nor your area of expertise.

- If necessary, consult with the school counseling or social work staff, the school psychologist, or the pupil personnel team.

Low Activity Level

Why Students
May Exhibit This Behavior

ACADEMIC Students who are failing in school can become very nervous and anxious because they know they are not doing as well as everyone else. Anxiety and tension can become manifested in a low activity level when students have given up and no longer feel they can succeed.

ENVIRONMENTAL Some adolescents come from families in which everyone is a success. In such a situation, the adolescent feels pressure to do great things. When she can't do what she thinks the family wants or what she feels she must do to maintain status within the family, she learns to give up, and her activity level decreases. Other students live in homes where the activity level is very low. They see all family members with very little—if any—motivation and drive. Unfortunately, they imitate the behavior they observe at home.

INTELLECTUAL Students with limited intelligence may have very low activity levels. Their intellectual limitations prevent them from doing as well as others, and they can suffer from a sense of failure. They begin to give up and eventually exhibit little energy.

MEDICAL Certain biochemical problems may lead to a low energy level. Also, the side effects of some medications can include fatigue, drowsiness, and decreased energy.

PSYCHOLOGICAL A very low activity level is one of the classic signs of depression. When adolescents are depressed, their energy becomes very limited. Their feelings of sadness about certain issues create states of learned helplessness, in which energy becomes depleted and drained. Also, anxiety and nervousness about life events can diminish energy. Psychologically, a low activity level can be a sign that a student is feeling unsure of herself and is expressing this feeling in behavioral ways.

SOCIAL Some students have a low activity level because they are not accepted by their peers or they lack social skills that may earn them positive reinforcement. They may want to fit in with the crowd but be unable to do so. They become isolated and withdraw from social activities. The energy for involvement they may once have had is no longer available.

What to Do

- Ask the school nurse if any medical conditions or factors (e.g., medication) might be contributing to the student's low activity level.

- Remember that a low activity level may fulfill a protective function for a student. Therefore, attempting to force her into a social situation will probably only create tremendous conflict, anxiety, and tension.

- Ask the school psychologist whether there are any particular circumstances underlying the student's low activity level (e.g., home issues, trauma, previous academic failure).

- Help the student feel more comfortable and confident by providing a foundation of successful experiences as well as the social tools she needs to be an active participant in the classroom.

- Meet with the student privately in a comfortable setting. Explain that you are aware of her difficulty in academic and/or social situations and that you want to help.

- Have the student work in groups so that the group energy creates excitement for her. Have the groups work on simple goal-oriented tasks that will ensure success. This will give the student the feeling of belonging and group accomplishment.

- Provide the student with a variety of small-group activities so that she has the opportunity to work with all members of her class. (Assign the groups and monitor their interactions to ensure protection and success.)

- Consult with the school counseling or social work staff or the school psychologist about the possibility of including the student in a social skills group or setting up a behavior modification program for her.

- If the problem is severe and persists, consult with the school's pupil personnel team.

Verbal Aggression

Why Students
May Exhibit This Behavior

ACADEMIC   Poor academic performance may cause some students to lash out verbally at others. Their inability to succeed in school becomes overwhelming, and they displace their anger through verbal means.

ENVIRONMENTAL   Unfortunately, some adolescents are verbally aggressive because of inappropriate parental modeling. They see parents being verbally aggressive toward each other and other family members. This is all they have learned about how to handle difficult situations, and they imitate this approach.

INTELLECTUAL   Intelligence involves many verbal qualities. Students with below-average intelligence may not be able to express their needs and wants in a socially appropriate manner and may instead release their feelings through verbal aggression.

LINGUISTIC   Students with language difficulties or those for whom the language of instruction is not the first language may be very frustrated with school. Lacking in language skills or just having trouble with language processing, they may become extremely upset. Often they will not know how to deal with the ensuing tension and will resort to abusive or harsh language to express their feelings.

MEDICAL   A student with a medical condition may feel as though life has treated him unfairly and may take out his anger and frustration through verbal aggression.

PERCEPTUAL   Perceptual problems can lead to great frustration in all areas of life. For some students with such problems, verbal aggression is the only way they know how to handle their anger.

PSYCHOLOGICAL   Some students have psychological problems that cause them to be very hostile and aggressive. They have "short fuses" and tend to lash out at others the moment something bothers them. Often this behavior is due to lack of restraint and inability to control their emotions.

SOCIAL   Some students do not know how to interact or compromise with others. When they cannot do as they wish, they become very upset and/or hostile. They may then express these feelings through verbal aggression.

What to Do

- Remain calm and intervene immediately before the verbal aggression escalates into a serious situation.

- Discuss the situation with the student; explain what is and is not appropriate in the classroom. Review the class rules and explain why they are necessary. Explain the consequences of continued verbal aggression.

- Speak to the student about his impact on others. Explain how his behavior is creating numerous problems not only for himself but for all others in the classroom.

- Ask the school psychologist whether the student is currently facing any underlying familial or emotional problems.

- If necessary, confer with the parents about the student's aggressive behavior.

- Help the student verbalize his feelings. Often adolescents who are aggressive may have difficulties verbalizing what they are feeling, and they then act out these frustrations through aggressive acts. Provide appropriate emotional labels that may identify what the student is feeling. Once students have the appropriate labels for their feelings, they can communicate their frustrations rather than act them out.

- Be sure not to put the student down in front of his classmates. This will only embarrass the student and keep him just as angry, if not make him angrier.

- Consult with the school counseling or social work staff or the school psychologist about the possibility of setting up a behavior modification program for the student.

- If the problem is severe and persists, consult the school's pupil personnel team.

Anger and Annoyance

Why Students
May Exhibit This Behavior

ACADEMIC   Academic frustration and failure over a period of time can reduce a student's sense of self-worth and confidence and can drain energy necessary for patience and motivation. As a result, the student may lose perspective and become angry when faced with a real or perceived academic failure situation.

ENVIRONMENTAL   Students whose parents are overreactive, highly critical, or easily agitated may exhibit the same behaviors in school. They learn to deal with frustration in this manner and respond to many situations with anger or annoyance.

INTELLECTUAL   Students with limited intellectual capacity may exhibit anger or annoyance because of ongoing frustration due to their limitations.

LINGUISTIC   See *Academic.*

MEDICAL   A tendency to become angry or easily annoyed may be due to a chemical imbalance. If a student has a medical, neurological, or organic problem, she may exhibit lower levels of tolerance than do other students.

PERCEPTUAL   See *Academic.*

PSYCHOLOGICAL   Students who are vulnerable as a result of a dysfunctional or abusive home life may use anger or annoyance as a defense against the perceived possibility of criticism, rejection, or devaluation. Also, students who exhibit these symptoms may be suffering from oppositional defiant disorder.

SOCIAL   Social fears, poor social skills, or social rejection may reduce a student's sense of self-worth and cause her to become angry or easily annoyed.

What to Do

- Try to determine what, exactly, is angering the student. Often there is a specific event or task, or another student, that triggers the reaction.

- Talk with the student privately. Describe what you are observing, and have her explain why she is so easily angered or annoyed.

- After listening to the student, do whatever you can to make the necessary changes in the classroom so that she can function more easily. For example, seat the student at the front of the classroom so that you can better observe her behaviors and defuse her anger. Or seat the student next to a classmate who you know will not provoke feelings of anger or hostility.

- For your own safety and for liability reasons, do not leave this student alone with other students. Be sure that supervision is constant.

- If the student cannot maintain self-control, remove her from the environment for the safety of the other students.

- If necessary, contact the parents to see if there is anything happening at home that is creating the anger in the student.

- Let the student know that if she feels an outburst is imminent, she does not have to participate in class activities at that moment. Devise an acceptable way for her to deal with such a situation, and create a signal she can give you when she feels anger building.

- Consult with the school counseling or social work staff or the school psychologist about appropriate intervention. Possibilities include a behavior modification plan, coping skills training, and group work.

- If the problem is severe and persists, consult the school's pupil personnel team.

Anxiety

Why Students
May Exhibit This Behavior

ACADEMIC   Students who lack academic skills may feel anxiety when they realize that they cannot succeed as others do in school. Academic failure can create a state of high tension because school plays such an important role in a student's everyday life.

ENVIRONMENTAL   Adolescents may be anxious because they live in homes where there are very serious problems: neglect or abuse, bitter divorce battles, and the like. Others may believe that their parents expect them to be perfect and experience serious anxiety about possible failure.

INTELLECTUAL   Students with limited intelligence may be very anxious because they cannot do things as well or as fast as everyone else. This can create an anticipation of embarrassment, which leads to anxiety.

LINGUISTIC   Students with language difficulties may be very nervous and frightened when they anticipate having to speak in front of the class. The anxiety provoked by their language problems may lead them to withdraw altogether from participation for fear of appearing foolish.

MEDICAL   In some cases, students have anxiety problems because of biochemical imbalances. Also, certain medications may make students feel jittery and anxious.

PERCEPTUAL   Students with perceptual difficulties may be very anxious when they anticipate having to read or write in front of the class. Like language problems, perceptual problems can cause students eventually to withdraw altogether from participation.

PSYCHOLOGICAL   Inadequate emotional development owing to parental rejection, lack of emotional involvement, favoritism toward another sibling, marital tension, and so on can make a student very anxious. Almost always, whenever there is anxiety, psychological factors play a critical role.

SOCIAL   Students may be anxious because they lack friends and do not fit in with the crowd. They feel unaccepted and become anxious whenever they anticipate interacting with their peers.

What to Do

- Remember that an adolescent suffering from anxiety is feeling very unsure of himself and the situation. Therefore, attempting to force him into particular situations will only heighten the conflict, anxiety, and tension.

- Ask the school psychologist whether there are any particular circumstances behind the anxiety (e.g., home issues, trauma, previous academic failure).

- Understand that a student experiencing anxiety must be made comfortable in the classroom. At times, making him comfortable may be like coaxing a frightened turtle out of its shell. It requires patience.

- Help the student gradually build confidence. The anxious student needs a foundation of successful experiences as well as appropriate social tools in order to be an active participant in the classroom.

- Speak with the student privately in a comfortable setting. Explain that you are aware of his difficulty and want to help.

- Have the student work in groups so that he can build confidence in the classroom. Assign the groups simple goal-oriented tasks that will ensure success. This will let the student experience the feeling of belonging and group accomplishment.

- Provide a variety of small-group activities so that the student has the opportunity to work with all the members of his class. For instance, have the student work on one project with one small group, then work on another project with a different small group. (Assign the groups and monitor them to ensure success.)

- Consult with the school counseling or social work staff or the school psychologist about the possibility of including the student in a social skills group or setting up a behavior modification program for him.

- If the problem is severe and persists, consult with the school's pupil personnel team.

Argumentativeness

Why Students
May Exhibit This Behavior

ACADEMIC Students who do not experience academic success may feel very stressed. The tension persists as they realize that they cannot succeed as others do in school. Academic failure then becomes problematic: The student decides to take an angry stance and may argue about the need, amount, purpose, and importance of what is required.

ENVIRONMENTAL Adolescents may be argumentative because they see such behavior exhibited at home. They may see their parents fighting frequently and imitate this behavior. In other cases, students who are afraid of their parents decide to adopt an argumentative stance with other authority figures because they cannot do so at home.

INTELLECTUAL Students with limited intelligence may be very argumentative because they cannot do things as well or as fast as their peers and suffer from anticipated embarrassment and insecurity. More often than not, by taking an argumentative approach, these students are simply masking their feelings of anger about their lack of ability.

LINGUISTIC Students with language difficulties may be very nervous and scared when they anticipate having to speak in front of the class. They may act on their anxieties by taking an argumentative stance. By constantly arguing with the teacher, such a student is actually just trying to avoid doing something that she does not want to do.

PERCEPTUAL Students with perceptual difficulties may be very nervous and scared when they anticipate having to read or write in front of the class. They may become argumentative to avoid having to perform.

PSYCHOLOGICAL Some adolescents may be very argumentative because they suffer from low self-esteem. They do not know any way to deal with their insecurities other than by being argumentative. In actuality, this behavior only masks doubts and fears.

SOCIAL Adolescents may be argumentative because they want to be the leaders of their social groups. Furthermore, some do not take well to criticism from their peers; they will argue over everything if they do not get what they want or hear what they want to hear.

What to Do

- Remain calm and intervene immediately before the student's argumentativeness escalates into a serious situation.

- Discuss the situation with the student; explain what is and is not appropriate in the classroom. Explain the consequences of a continued argumentative approach. Be sure not to put the student down in front of her classmates. This will only embarrass her and may even aggravate her anger.

- A student who is argumentative may be fighting off feelings of insignificance. In this case, assign the student a position of leadership for some in-school group activity. This places emphasis on group responsibility and gives the student a significant feeling of empowerment.

- Speak to the student about her impact on others. Explain how her behavior is creating numerous problems not only for herself but for her classmates. Help the student to verbalize her feelings. Often, students who are argumentative have difficulties verbalizing what they are feeling, and they then act out their frustrations.

- Ask the school psychologist about possible underlying familial or emotional problems.

- If necessary, confer with the parents about the student's argumentative approach to handling issues.

- Consult with the school counseling or social work staff or the school psychologist about the possibility of setting up a behavior modification program for the student.

- If the problem is severe and persists, consult with the school's pupil personnel team.

Need for Immediate Attention

Why Students
May Exhibit This Behavior

ACADEMIC   Students who have academic difficulties may not know how to wait for the teacher to attend to their needs. They may be so insecure that they feel the only way to keep pace is to get immediate attention for whatever problems or questions they are facing at the moment.

ENVIRONMENTAL   The need for immediate attention may stem from a lack of nurturance or a privation of attention at home. It can also be a manifestation of panic behavior brought on by abuse, neglect, or lack of parental involvement.

INTELLECTUAL   Students with limited intellectual ability may lack the social awareness that comes with social maturity. They may compensate for their feelings of inadequacy by constantly demanding reassurance.

LINGUISTIC   See *Intellectual.*

MEDICAL   Some adolescents with medical problems may need immediate attention because of specific physical difficulties. Such adolescents may not be able to wait until the teacher has time to help. For example, a wheelchair user may need immediate assistance to visit the bathroom, to reach something, and so on.

PERCEPTUAL   See *Intellectual.*

PSYCHOLOGICAL   If the student's need for attention is not filled by significant individuals in his life, he experiences anxiety and then must seek to meet this need through any means possible. In his deprivation, he becomes like a starving person who acts to assuage his hunger without thought of consequences. His only goal in acting impulsively or seeking the spotlight is to reduce the tension. Outside the spotlight, the student feels insignificant.

SOCIAL   Social insecurities heightened at certain stages of development may cause students to demand immediate attention from peers. This excessive behavior stems from a fear of being rejected or seen as insignificant. The anxiety arising from the fear causes some students to seek constant reassurance from peers. However, it usually angers others, provoking real avoidance and rejection. This in turn heightens the anxiety of the student, who reacts by seeking more reassurance, creating a vicious cycle of rejection.

What to Do

- Explain to the student that you have a full class and cannot play favorites with anyone.

- Teach the student about patience and the need to wait his turn. Assure him that you will attend to him, though not at every moment when he wants attention.

- When the student demands attention, say, in a firm but compassionate tone, "Please wait. I'll be with you as soon as I can."

- If many students in the class have this same problem, give a lesson about keeping a safe and cooperative environment. Stress turn taking, sharing, and patience.

- Explain that everyone in the class is very important and that although you would like to help everyone, you have only two hands. Therefore, everyone must learn to be more independent.

- If the problem becomes serious, contact the parents to see if there is an underlying familial problem.

- Consult with the school counseling or social work staff or the school psychologist about the possibility of involving the student in individual or group therapy or setting up a behavior modification program for him.

- If the problem is serious and persists, consult with the school's pupil personnel team.

Attention Seeking

Why Students
May Exhibit This Behavior

ACADEMIC   Some students with academic problems feel the need to monopolize the teacher's attention, as well as the attention of their peers. They crave recognition because they are not succeeding in their schoolwork. They hope that being the center of attention will compensate for their academic inadequacies.

ENVIRONMENTAL   Some students do not get much attention at home, and their need for reinforcement is very high. They take this need into the classroom, where they try to occupy the spotlight. Conversely, some students are always the center of attention at home and thus expect to occupy the same place at school. This latter situation can be common with only children, who get 100 percent of parental attention.

INTELLECTUAL   Some students with limited intellectual ability try to compensate by being the center of attention. Students with high intellectual ability may monopolize attention because they want to be recognized for their intelligence.

LINGUISTIC   Some students have very strong verbal abilities. They speak quite clearly and with some eloquence. When they realize this strength, they begin wanting to be the center of attention because of the associated accolades.

MEDICAL   Sometimes students with medical problems have a legitimate need for more assistance to function well in the classroom. The situation becomes problematic when these students start to monopolize attention even when they do not need it.

PERCEPTUAL   See *Academic*.

PSYCHOLOGICAL   Students who always need to be the center of attention may have problems with self-esteem and self-confidence stemming from insecurities regarding their abilities in any number of life areas.

Social   There are students who need to be the center of attention simply because they absolutely love it. In fact, being the center of attention can make someone very popular if she can do it without being annoying. For example, being elected school president or becoming a class leader affords a student great social status and earns her the desired center of attention. Less appropriate attention-seeking behavior, likely the result of fear of being rejected or seen as insignificant, may cause the student to seek constant reassurance from peers. However, this usually angers others, provoking real avoidance and rejection. This response in turn heightens the anxiety of the student, who reacts by seeking more reassurance, creating a vicious cycle of rejection.

What to Do

- Keep in mind that the craving for attention may contain a message. This means that the student's real motive is not overt but is communicated indirectly through attention-seeking behavior.

- Recognize that in some cases the student's need for attention may not be the problem; the problem may lie in the choice of behaviors to derive attention.

- Ask the school psychologist if there are any underlying circumstances that might be creating this pattern of inappropriate behavior.

- Provide the student with controlled attention when she least expects it. For example, go to her or call her to your desk for reassurance or observation of a positive behavior. Let her know at the end of the day the things that you found to be most positive.

- Meet with the student individually and preempt inappropriate behavior. This means telling the student before she enters the room in the morning that you will no longer allow her to act inappropriately in the classroom and that there will be serious consequences if the behavior persists. The consequences should be determined prior to discussing the situation with the student.

- Students who are unresponsive to the preceding suggestions may have a more serious problem. If the problem continues, consult with the school counseling or social work staff, the school psychologist, or the pupil personnel team.

Short Attention Span

Why Students
May Exhibit This Behavior

ACADEMIC Many adolescents have great difficulty attending to tasks that are boring for them because they are not engaged in the subjects being taught. Work that is too difficult also may cause problems in attending to tasks.

ENVIRONMENTAL Some adolescents cannot attend to tasks because they have learned that inattention is acceptable. Their home lives may be characterized by constant disorganization and limited structure. They may be allowed to start things and not finish them, or they may never have been taught that life sometimes requires paying attention to things we don't like. As this behavior pattern carries over into all aspects of life, they develop short attention spans.

INTELLECTUAL Limited intelligence can hinder a student's ability to attend to a task. Conversely, a student with very high intelligence may also have great difficulty staying on task in school because he becomes rapidly bored in a classroom designed for average students.

LINGUISTIC Students who have trouble understanding language can have difficulties with schoolwork. Because it can take them much longer to read a passage or understand a lecture, they easily become frustrated and give up. They exhibit general inattention and specific lack of attention to the tasks at hand.

MEDICAL There are many different theories regarding the causes of inattention. The most prominent theory is that it is a neurological problem, specifically the result of attention deficit/hyperactivity disorder (AD/HD).

PERCEPTUAL When students do not see the world as others do, they can experience great frustration in academic work. Attempting to do the work but consistently falling short of success, they eventually become overwhelmed and unable to focus on anything—because even when they are focused, they do not succeed.

PSYCHOLOGICAL   Some students exhibit short attention spans because their inattentiveness brings them attention from authority figures. At school or at home, if the student consistently does not listen, the teacher and the parents focus all of their energy on correcting his behavior. This becomes psychologically reinforcing.

SOCIAL   Some adolescents cannot stay on task because they are completely absorbed in their social lives and social issues. They slight academic work not because of its difficulties but rather because their social preoccupation takes precedence, leaving no energy to focus on schoolwork.

What to Do

- Check with the school nurse and confer with the student's parents to rule out medical problems that could be causing the student's difficulty focusing on tasks.
- Try to limit auditory and visual stimuli in the classroom so that the student does not have too many things to focus on at one time.
- Talk with the student about why he feels that he has trouble staying on task.
- Give verbal praise when you notice the student on task, however briefly. This will help build his confidence.
- Try to get involved with the student's activities when he needs to stay on task. Your interaction with him may increase his chances of focusing.
- Have the student work in groups with others who you know have very good attention spans.
- Have the student write down (or write down for him) exactly what it is that he must do. Often students who cannot stay on task forget what they were required to do because they have been distracted by other stimuli. Having the directions written down enables the student to get back on track and maintain his original focus.

- Try to change the topics in the lesson as often as possible, although this may be difficult if you have a large number of students in your class. Find out how other teachers handle this situation.
- Seat the student in the front of the class so he will be less distracted by other stimuli within the room.
- Increase the number of hands-on tasks as opposed to straight academic work; try to incorporate more visuals within the classroom.
- Consider being more flexible. Being too rigid with a student who has a short attention span will only create conflict, anxiety, and tension on both your and the student's part.
- Call on the student more often than on others without making it too obvious. By keeping the student on his toes, you will increase his chances of staying focused.
- Offer the student extra help before or after school to deal with his attention problem.
- Consult with the school counseling or social work staff or the school psychologist about the possibility of setting up a behavior modification program for the student.
- If the problem is severe and persists, consult the pupil personnel team.

Tough Attitude

Why Students
May Exhibit This Behavior

ACADEMIC   In general, acting tough is an expression of frustration or insecurity on the part of adolescents. Adolescents who suffer from academic frustration may act tough because they cannot succeed as they know their peers can.

ENVIRONMENTAL   Some adolescents may act tough as a result of pressure or stressors experienced at home. These may include unrealistic expectations from parents, poor parenting skills, inability to live up to siblings' successes, or, in the extreme, abuse.

INTELLECTUAL   In some cases, limited intelligence can lead to tough behavior. Some students who feel very inadequate because of their limitations may feel they must find other ways to gain status—for example, by picking on other students who are not as strong as they.

LINGUISTIC   Students who have difficulty communicating as a result of linguistic limitations may release their frustrations through tough behavior, not words.

MEDICAL   Some students may act tough because they possess a truly aggressive tendency. Their aggressive behavior may be due to neurological impairment or chemical imbalance. In addition, some medications may increase aggressive tendencies, leading to the possibility for more aggressive behavior.

PERCEPTUAL   For students whose perceptions are different from others', frustration may result. Such students act tough to release their conflict, anxiety, and tension.

PSYCHOLOGICAL   Certain psychological factors (e.g., low self-esteem, anxiety, depressed mood) can create a state of inadequacy in some adolescents. They may deal with the resulting tension by acting out aggressively toward those less able than they.

SOCIAL Some students feel socially rejected, socially inadequate, and as though they do not fit in. They may deal with these feelings by acting tough in school. In addition, bullying behavior may serve to elevate one's status within the peer group.

What to Do

- The approach recommended has three parts:

  1. Meet with the adolescent privately to discuss the seriousness of the situation and the consequences if the behavior continues. Convey that although you understand she may have issues that cause her to act this way and that you will help her try to understand them, you will not tolerate the behavior. Keep in mind that acting tough is not a sign of strength but a sign of a fragile ego. Do not hesitate to establish yourself as the benevolent authority.

  2. Try to help the adolescent understand why she is acting tough. Encourage her to verbalize what she is feeling. If she is unable to verbalize, you may want to provide some labels for what she may be feeling. You might say, for example, that you have noticed that some adolescents act tough because they feel they are not doing well at school, have problems at home, or feel rejected by other students.

  3. Suggest alternate means of resolving future conflicts. Many students who consistently act tough know no other way to react to stressful situations. They may need to be taught other means of response.

- If this pattern is consistently displayed, confer with the student's parents to inform them of the situation and determine whether family factors play a part.

- If necessary, consult with the school counseling or social work staff, the school psychologist, or the pupil personnel team.

Frequent Bathroom Visits

Why Students
May Exhibit This Behavior

ACADEMIC   Students who make frequent trips to the bathroom may be acting out anxiety due to schoolwork. Nervousness, stress, and tension can create a state of physical discomfort that necessitates a bathroom visit. Sometimes, the fear of academic failure can be so severe that a student will get sick to the point of needing to urinate, defecate, or even vomit.

ENVIRONMENTAL   Adolescents who make frequent bathroom visits may have serious problems at home. Their parents may be upset with them, there may be contentiousness and impending divorce, they may be neglected or abused, and so on. The resultant overwhelming stress can create a state of physical discomfort that necessitates a bathroom visit. Sometimes, anxiety over home stressors is so severe that a student will get physically sick.

INTELLECTUAL   Students with limited intellectual ability may make frequent trips to the bathroom because they are not able to keep up with the class. Panic about inability to succeed despite great effort can create physical discomfort, which can necessitate a bathroom visit.

LINGUISTIC   Students with language difficulties may make frequent bathroom visits when they anticipate speaking in front of the class. Their trips to the bathroom may be avoidance behavior or may result from physical discomfort caused by nervousness. Sometimes, this anxiety over having to perform can be so severe that a student will become physically ill in anticipation of the event.

MEDICAL   Some medical problems can create the necessity to go to the bathroom particularly often. This can be the case if a student has a disorder of the bladder, colon, or kidneys.

PERCEPTUAL   See *Linguistic*.

PSYCHOLOGICAL   There are many possible psychological reasons why students need to make frequent trips to the bathroom. However, barring any serious medical condition, most students who manifest this behavior are experiencing some form of anxiety. It can stem from any of the situations previously discussed. However, it is important to understand that this psychological pain creates real tension, causing physical discomfort to the point where a trip to the bathroom is very much needed.

SOCIAL   The school bathroom can be a place to socialize, and students may go there frequently to rendezvous or hang out with their friends. Students may also be involved with illegal activities. They may be in the bathroom smoking, buying drugs, or engaging in some other form of destructive behavior.

What to Do

- Contact the school nurse and/or the parents to determine if there are any underlying medical problems.
- If no medical problems exist, then you can take the following steps:
  1. Discuss the situation with the student and find out why the student needs to visit the bathroom so often.
  2. Encourage the student to limit fluid intake during the course of the day.
  3. Do not give out bathroom passes during class lessons.
  4. Set times during the day when students are not allowed to go to the bathroom unless it is absolutely necessary.
  5. Establish a sign-out sheet for the bathroom. Allow students only a reasonable number of bathroom visits during the day (except in case of emergency).
- If necessary, consult with the school counseling or social work staff, the school psychologist, or the pupil personnel team.

Blaming Others

ACADEMIC   Frustration commonly leads to anger. Students who suffer from academic frustration may displace their anger toward others in the form of blame because they cannot succeed at schoolwork as they know others can.

ENVIRONMENTAL   Adolescents may blame others because of stressors experienced at home. These may include unrealistic expectations from parents, inability to live up to a sibling's success or—in the most serious of cases—physical abuse.

INTELLECTUAL   In some cases, limited intelligence can lead to blaming behavior. Some students may feel inadequate as a result of their limitations, become upset, and externalize their problems by blaming others for their limitations rather than dealing with them.

LINGUISTIC   Students with language limitations who have difficulty communicating may release their frustrations through their words. For example, if the student comes from a home where English is not the first language, he may blame others, especially his parents, for his language problems.

MEDICAL   Adolescents with medical conditions may blame others for their problems. The parents may bear the brunt of this blame. An adolescent may have great difficulty dealing with the fact that he has a medical problem and, rather than concentrate on coping with it, may spend time blaming the world.

PERCEPTUAL   Some students have difficulty perceiving the world as others do, and high frustration may be the result. This frustration can lead them to blame others for all of their problems, especially when they feel that no one understands them and what they are experiencing.

PSYCHOLOGICAL Certain psychological states (e.g., low self-esteem, anxiety, depressed mood) can create feelings of inadequacy in some students and raise their levels of tension. They may feel as though they have been "dealt a bad hand" in life and may act out their tensions by blaming others for their problems.

SOCIAL Some students may feel rejected and socially inadequate if they do not fit in. They may act out the resultant frustrations by blaming others for all of their problems. Unable to function socially as their peers do, they blame the world for their problems and complain about others rather than focusing on their own problems and how to address them.

What to Do

- Talk with the student privately and discuss what you have been noticing about his behavior. Ask the student his opinion of the behavior; get his perspective.

- Determine whether or not the student realizes what he is doing. Sometimes, the student will have a thin layer of denial and, when confronted, will own up to the behavior. If this is the case, the situation may be easier to address. However, another student may have a deeper level of denial; in that case, do not push for insight or admission. Instead, talk with the school psychologist because this denial may be covering a more fragile ego.

- If the student understands what he is doing but is not sure how to change it, explain to him why his behavior is detrimental to his making friends and succeeding in school. The student needs to become aware of how his behavior affects others.

- Try to offer the student ideas and options for what to do when he has the urge to blame others. For instance, have the student sit closer to you in the classroom so that he may feel more secure and connected. Also, let him know that if he feels like blaming others, he may want to come to you first and discuss his motives.

- Try to discern patterns in the behavior. There may be a theme connecting the issues, experiences, or situations that give rise to the behavior because blaming others is an attempt to refocus the spotlight, especially in situations in which the student feels inadequate.

- Give verbal praise when you notice an instance when the student could have blamed others but used some other method to solve the problem. Let him know that you are proud of his behavior and that you appreciate his effort to handle the situation in a constructive way.

- If the situation does not improve over time, confer with the parents about possible underlying circumstances that may be causing the student to blame others.

- If necessary, consult the school counseling or social work staff, the school psychologist, or the pupil personnel team.

Body Piercing

Why Students
May Exhibit This Behavior

ACADEMIC   Adolescents who engage in body piercing may be doing so because they are performing poorly in academics. When they feel out of control in terms of their schoolwork, they may turn to body piercing because it is something they can control. In a sense, body piercing is a way of dealing with insecurity and regaining inner control.

ENVIRONMENTAL   When difficulties arise at home, adolescents may pierce body parts as a way of rebelling. Their dissatisfaction with the ways things are at home and their inability to influence the situation create discomfort. Body piercing is a way to get back at their parents for what they feel is an unfair way of life.

INTELLECTUAL   See *Academic*.

PSYCHOLOGICAL   Body piercing may be an expression of depression, anxiety, or insecurity. Body piercing is a way to establish control and maintain a sense of self, which adolescents may be unable to accomplish verbally.

SOCIAL   Whether through the ear, belly button, tongue, or eyebrow, body piercing has become increasingly popular. If an adolescent has a group of friends who pierce certain parts of their bodies, she may want to do likewise to avoid appearing different.

What to Do

Whether or not you approve of body piercing, the fact is that as a teacher you have no legal responsibility or right to tell an adolescent what to do with her body unless she is truly hurting herself. If you find the situation troublesome, you may discuss it with the principal, or the counseling or social work staff, but ultimately there is little you can do about it.

Bothering Others

Why Students
May Exhibit This Behavior

ACADEMIC   Students who do not understand the assigned work or feel academically inadequate may express their discomfort by attempting to stop others from working so that they do not feel so different. In other cases, students who are confused about academic tasks may vent their frustration by bothering others.

ENVIRONMENTAL   Students who feel they are not receiving enough attention at home may seek it at any opportunity. In the classroom, such students may feel insignificant and crave attention to ease their tension. Because they are driven by their tension, their judgment is impaired, and they will engage in any behavior that reduces the tension, without regard for the circumstances, the rights of others, or the consequences.

INTELLECTUAL   Students with limited intellectual abilities may lose focus quickly and bother others in immature attempts to engage them in play rather than work.

LINGUISTIC   See *Academic.*

MEDICAL   Bothering others may be indicative of attention deficit/hyperactivity disorder. Students with AD/HD exhibit several symptoms—including inattention, hyperactivity, and impulsivity—and it is not uncommon for them to persist in bothering others at inopportune times.

PERCEPTUAL   Adolescents with perceptual difficulties may not be capable of the internal processing necessary to perceive a behavior as situationally inappropriate. They may perceive themselves as behaving acceptably.

PSYCHOLOGICAL   Students who are highly anxious, angry, overwhelmed, or oppositional and defiant (unable to follow rules, apt to intrude on the rights and properties of others) will bother others quite frequently. The determining factor here is the student's lack of internal controls and recognition of boundaries. Some students who lack internal control are unable to set their own boundaries but may respond to external control from teachers and other authority figures. In more serious cases, students do not respond to any external control exerted by any authority figure (e.g., the principal). Such students may require a very restrictive educational setting.

SOCIAL   Some students who have an exaggerated need for acceptance will continually bother students whose notice they wish to attract. This behavior is self-defeating because it commonly elicits negative feedback from the other students or the teacher.

What to Do

- Talk with the student about what you are observing. Explain that his behavior in the classroom is becoming problematic and that it must stop.

- Give the student the opportunity to explain his side of the story. Find out why he is bothering others. Is it because he does not understand assignments, needs extra attention, and so on?

- Involve yourself with the student as much as possible to take his focus off the other students.

- Seat the student next to a peer who can help him out and who is also compassionate and understanding.

- Let the student participate as much as possible in class discussions so that he feels that he is getting the attention he needs.

- If the student is consistently bothering the same people, remove him from their area. If necessary, seat him closer to you so that you can keep an eye on him.

- If the situation warrants it, contact the parents to find out whether the behavior is specific to school or occurs at home as well.

- When the student is not bothering others, praise him for his constructive behavior.

- When the student is bothering others, act immediately to let him know that the behavior is not acceptable.
- If necessary, consult with the school counseling or social work staff, the school psychologist, or the pupil personnel team.

Boy or Girl Craziness

Why Students
May Exhibit This Behavior

ACADEMIC   Students with academic difficulties may need help from others. Girlfriends or boyfriends may represent that reliable source of assistance with class work or homework.

ENVIRONMENTAL   Some adolescents may be boy or girl crazy because they see similar behavior modeled at home. For example, a girl with older sisters may hear them talking constantly about boys. Also, students with divorced parents may see their parents dating, and they may become aware of dating relationships earlier than their peers.

MEDICAL   Some adolescents go through puberty much earlier than others. The change in hormones can create new and exciting feelings. These physiological changes give rise to new emotions pertaining to sexuality.

PSYCHOLOGICAL   Some adolescents feel the need to be boy or girl crazy to compensate for something they consciously or unconsciously feel is missing in their lives—more often than not, love and attention. They cling to members of the opposite sex not necessarily because it feels right but rather because having a girlfriend or boyfriend involves giving and receiving affection and "love." Their lack of confidence in their ability to be alone strengthens the need for opposite-sex relationships.

SOCIAL   Having a girlfriend or boyfriend, especially at an early age, can confer great status in the elementary grades. Early dating is likely to lead to popularity within the school. This social status is something that many students desire, and they decide to pursue it by acting boy or girl crazy.

What to Do

- Most of the time, students' boy- or girl-crazy behavior does not interfere with a teacher's work in the classroom. It does not often warrant too much concern. However, if you find that it is a problem in your classroom, we suggest the following measures:

1. Plan a group lesson to discuss appropriate boy-girl behavior.
2. Explain that friendship does not have to involve hugging and kissing.
3. Give creative writing assignments that invite students to express their feelings about boy-girl relationships.
4. Invite a professional within the school to speak to the class about the nature of relationships and friendships in elementary school.
5. Talk to students privately to discuss their feelings and how they should be acting in school.

- If the problem is severe and persists, consult with the school counseling or social work staff, the school psychologist, or the pupil personnel team.

Bullying

Why Students
May Exhibit This Behavior

ACADEMIC   In general, bullying behavior is an expression of some frustration or insecurity on the part of the perpetrator. Students who experience academic frustration may bully other students because they cannot succeed at schoolwork as they know others can. They are displacing their anger toward those who are weaker.

ENVIRONMENTAL   Some adolescents may become bullies as a result of stressors experienced at home. These may include unrealistic expectations from parents, inability to live up to a sibling's success, or—in the most serious cases—physical abuse. Adolescents may also imitate the aggressive behavior of parents or siblings, or bullying actions may be supported by cultural or community norms.

INTELLECTUAL   Students with limited intelligence may feel very inadequate and may seek to gain status by picking on students who are weaker than they.

LINGUISTIC   Students who have difficulty communicating as a result of language limitations may vent their frustrations through bullying behavior instead of through words.

MEDICAL   Some adolescents may be predisposed toward aggression due to neurological impairments or chemical imbalances. Also, some medications may increase aggressive tendencies, possibly leading to bullying behavior.

PERCEPTUAL   Students who have difficulty perceiving the world as others do may experience frustration. They become the school bullies to release conflict, anxiety, and tension.

PSYCHOLOGICAL   Certain psychological states (e.g., low self-esteem, anxiety, depressed mood) can create a feeling of inadequacy in some students and increase their levels of tension. They may attempt to relieve the tension through aggressive behavior toward smaller, weaker, nonthreatening peers. They become bullies not from high confidence but rather from insecurities that need to be vented.

SOCIAL Some adolescents may feel socially rejected and socially inadequate; they feel that they do not fit in. They may act out their frustrations physically by bullying. Also, bullying may be a sign of status and power within a peer group. Adolescents may become bullies to get peer recognition and show their friends just how "powerful" they are.

What to Do

- We suggest a three-step approach for dealing with bullying:

  1. Set boundaries around the inappropriate behavior. Start by talking privately with the student. Keeping in mind that bullying behavior is a sign not of strength but rather of a fragile ego, do not hesitate to establish yourself as the benevolent authority. Discuss the seriousness of the situation and the consequences if it continues. Make clear that although you understand that certain issues may be prompting the student's behavior—and you will help her try to understand them—you will not tolerate the behavior.

  2. Try to understand the behavior and help the student understand it. Invite her to verbalize what she is feeling and why she behaves as she does. If she is unable to label her feelings, you may want to provide her with some labels. For example, you may want to say that you have seen other students bully because they felt they were not doing well in school, had problems at home, or felt rejected by other students.

  3. Help the student change the behavior. Suggest alternate means of resolving future conflicts. Many students who persist in bullying know no other way to handle difficult and stressful situations.

- If bullying is a consistent pattern of behavior, talk to the school psychologist about setting up a meeting with the parent(s) or developing a behavioral contract for the student.
- If the problem is severe and persists, consult with the school's pupil personnel team.

Cheating

ACADEMIC Cheating is often a cover-up for academic weakness. Students who fear being seen as academically inadequate by their teacher or—more important—by their peers will often cheat to protect their fragile egos. They believe that because they cannot succeed on their own, their only chance is to cheat.

ENVIRONMENTAL Cheating may be an attempt to avoid severe negative parental reactions associated with expectations the student feels he cannot meet, abuse, comparison or competition with siblings, or other family factors.

INTELLECTUAL Students with limited intellectual abilities may cheat because they know that they cannot do as well as other students without extra "help." In their minds, the only way to succeed is to cheat.

LINGUISTIC See *Academic*.

MEDICAL Students with medical problems may miss a great deal of school. Excessive absence can create real anxiety and tension when it comes to turning in assignments, keeping up in class, or taking quizzes and tests. Students thus affected may feel that the only way to succeed is to cheat.

PERCEPTUAL See *Academic*.

PSYCHOLOGICAL Cheating can be the result of high anxiety or a pathological aspect of a student's personality. The latter possibility is more serious and may require professional intervention. It means that the student cannot differentiate between cheating and honesty and truly believes that what he is doing is acceptable even though reality presents a different picture. In other cases, students may cheat impulsively, not considering consequences, and may feel guilt afterward.

SOCIAL   Students may cheat to gain status and acceptance within a peer group.

What to Do

- First, obtain complete information about the situation to avoid making false accusations.

- If you believe that a student has cheated, speak to him privately to avoid embarrassing him. If you address the matter in front of anyone—student or adult—you increase the chances of the student's lying to you because he will not want to be publicly humiliated.

- If you are reasonably sure that cheating has taken place, do not use entrapment. In other words, do not try to trick the student into admitting what he has done.

- Be diplomatic, clear, and direct in confronting the student with what you know to be the facts. Speak calmly but be firm to show the student that you are serious.

- After explaining your point of view, ask the student if he wants to rethink what was done. Don't put him on the spot if there is no immediate response. Say, "We will talk about this again some time today when you are ready, but we will definitely talk about it today."

- If the student admits to cheating, say that you appreciate his honesty, and then tell him what the consequences will be. The consequences should be appropriate and predetermined.

- If the student does not admit to cheating, you must act on the overwhelming evidence. Tell the student that the evidence indicates that he has indeed cheated and has violated class rules, then administer the consequences.

Not Handing In Class Work

Why Students
May Exhibit This Behavior

ACADEMIC   The many possible academic reasons students may avoid handing in class work can be grouped into two categories. First, they may find the work too difficult and no longer worth the effort. Second, they may lack motivation, whether because of boredom, difficulty sustaining effort, or some other factor.

ENVIRONMENTAL   Many environmental factors can lead adolescents to avoid handing in their work. For instance, they may lack parental supervision, the family may not reinforce the value of education, there may be family problems, or the home environment may not be conducive to studying.

INTELLECTUAL   Students with limited intellectual ability may be unable to complete class work as fast as their peers. Eventually they become overwhelmingly frustrated and give up. Conversely, students with high intelligence may stop doing class work if they see no purpose in routine practice of skills and knowledge they have already mastered.

LINGUISTIC   Some students may have difficulty either understanding language or expressing themselves verbally. The assignments may overwhelm them. They avoid handing in work altogether because, regardless of their effort, they see themselves as destined to fail.

MEDICAL   Some students may not hand in their class work because medical problems such as visual or hearing impairments, brain damage, or nervous system injury have prevented them from completing it.

PERCEPTUAL   Some students have great difficulty decoding and encoding words. The classic example is the dyslexic student. For such students, class work can be an absolute nightmare. What would take most students an hour takes these students 5 to 6 hours, and they still do not finish their assignments. Frustration escalates to the point that they see no purpose in doing class work.

PSYCHOLOGICAL   There are many possible psychological reasons students do not hand in class work. First, they may not be up to the responsibility and demands of school and feel highly frustrated as a result. Second, they may be engaging in a form of passive-aggressive behavior to upset their parents and/or teachers. Finally, they may be seeking negative attention by not doing certain things that they know are important to the authority figures in their lives.

SOCIAL   Some students may fail to hand in class work because they are too involved with their friends and social activities and put social life before academics. Other students may be responding to a peer group opinion that schoolwork is not "cool" to do.

What to Do

- Talk privately with the student about why she is not completing class work. Ask if she understands the directions for assignments. Many students require clarification.

- Ask the student what she can do to get the assignments completed. Do not criticize or be harsh; rather, assure the student that you want to help her.

- Explain the importance of doing class work and completing it on time.

- With the student, figure out what motivations and reinforcers will work for her.

- Explain to the student that if her behavior continues, there will be negative consequences. Determine the consequences beforehand, and convey them clearly to the student.

- Pair the student with a classmate who will model the desired behavior.

- Contact the parents to see if there are any circumstances underlying the student's problems. Try to be solution oriented and avoid blaming: The parents themselves may be frustrated with the student's behavior. Work with the parents to come up with a plan. Send daily notes home to the parents to explain what the student has done and what is due the next day.

- If necessary, consult with the school counseling or social work staff, the school psychologist, or the pupil personnel team.

Clowning

Why Students
May Exhibit This Behavior

ACADEMIC   Students who feel academically insecure may become class clowns in hopes of diverting attention from their academic inadequacies. In some cases, the student hopes to be removed from the class so she does not have to face ridicule or embarrassment over academic failure.

ENVIRONMENTAL   Students may become class clowns as a result of family interactions involving humor. In some cases, students are not provided the necessary boundaries or structure and may hence be unable to distinguish appropriate exhibition from inappropriate exhibition of humor.

INTELLECTUAL   Students may use humor to divert attention away from limited intellectual abilities. Humor may also give them a platform for feeling adequate.

MEDICAL   Attention deficit/hyperactivity disorder (AD/HD) may result in a student's using inappropriate humor because she may have difficulty observing boundaries. Inappropriate use of humor may be only one of several inappropriate behaviors exhibited by students with this disorder.

PERCEPTUAL   See *Academic.*

PSYCHOLOGICAL   A need for attention brought on by a lack of attention at home can result in clowning behavior. A student who uses humor in an appropriate manner and at an appropriate time does not have this problem. On the other hand, the one who uses humor at the wrong time and place is motivated more by neurotic need and anxiety than by a desire to be funny. The level of anxiety can be seen in the student's inability to discriminate between the appropriate and the inappropriate.

SOCIAL   Humor can gain a student social status and reinforcement. This reinforcement can be very powerful, and the need to be in the spotlight can overshadow negative implications or consequences.

What to Do

- Keep in mind that the class clown may be sending a message. The student's real motive is not overt but is being communicated indirectly through humor.

- Ask the school psychologist whether there are any life circumstances that might be creating this pattern of inappropriate behavior.

- Confer with the parents if necessary.

- In order to deal with this pattern, you must understand that the student's need for attention is not the problem. The problem is the student's choice of behaviors to elicit attention. Therefore, you need to take the following steps:

  1. Give the student controlled attention when she least expects it. For example, go to her or call her to your desk for reassurance or observation of a positive behavior. Let her know at the end of the day the most positive behaviors that you observed.

  2. Provide the student with controlled activities that will allow for social presentation of her humor. For example, allot a time at the end of the day when she can tell the class an appropriate joke or story. This scheduled time may satisfy the student's need for group attention.

  3. Meet with the student privately and preempt the inappropriate behavior. Tell her before she enters class in the morning that you will not allow her to behave inappropriately and that there will be serious consequences if she violates the rules. (These consequences should be determined beforehand.) Explain that you expect cooperation and that, if necessary, you will provide the student with other outlets for humor. You may need to repeat this process several times to reinforce your seriousness.

- The foregoing suggestions assume that the student may be able to exercise humor appropriately in a controlled setting. However, if the student's sense of humor is highly inappropriate or immature, or does not respond to the limits you establish, you should refer her to the school counseling or social work staff, the school psychologist, or the pupil personnel team.

Clumsiness

Why Students
May Exhibit This Behavior

ACADEMIC See *Psychological.*

ENVIRONMENTAL See *Psychological.*

INTELLECTUAL One aspect of intelligence concerns spatial perceptual abilities. A student who is weak in this area may exhibit clumsy and awkward behavior.

MEDICAL Some medical problems may cause a student to be clumsy. Such problems can range from the minimal to the severe (for example, cerebral palsy or spina bifida).

PERCEPTUAL If a student sees things backward or cannot discriminate between figure and ground, his sense of balance may be affected. He may be very clumsy in activities that are routine for most students.

PSYCHOLOGICAL Some students pretend to be clumsy because it elicits laughter from friends and family and earns them the attention that they are seeking. In other cases, anxiety, which creates fear and tension, can lead to clumsy and awkward movement.

SOCIAL Some students become very anxious or nervous when involved in social activities. Their fears and insecurities cause clumsiness in movements and speech.

What to Do

- Consult with the physical therapist or occupational therapist within the school to find out if the student has medical problems of which you are not aware.

- Provide a safe environment within the classroom for the student. In his area, separate the desks a little more so that moving around is easier.

- Never bring the student's clumsiness to the attention of the class. Most likely, the behavior is involuntary, and the student should never be made the object of ridicule.

- Provide activities in the classroom that can help the student improve motor skills. Your school's physical or occupational therapist can suggest appropriate activities.

- A student who is clumsy may simply be rushing his activities, thinking of too many things at one time. If this is happening, encourage the student to slow down and explain the importance of taking his time.

- If you feel the student is acting clumsy simply to get attention (and this is something you must be very sure about; if you are wrong, it can damage the student's self-esteem), speak with the student privately and explain that his attention-seeking behavior will not be tolerated. Ask him why he behaves as he does and what he hopes to accomplish with this behavior.

- If the problem is severe and persists, consult with the school counseling or social work staff, the school psychologist, or the pupil personnel team.

Inappropriate Comments and Noises

Why Students
May Exhibit This Behavior

ACADEMIC Inability to complete or understand academic assignments may trigger acute anxiety in some students, and the resulting nervous tension may be released through inappropriate noises or comments.

ENVIRONMENTAL Some adolescents who make inappropriate noises or comments may come from homes where parents do not set boundaries or establish consequences for inappropriate actions. Others may feel that they do not receive enough attention and may use inappropriate sounds or comments to get into the spotlight.

INTELLECTUAL In a student with low intellectual functioning, inappropriate utterances may be symptomatic of overall immature behavior.

MEDICAL Inappropriate, unusual, or unexplained utterances or sounds may be an indication of Tourette's syndrome, a neurological disorder that appears to be genetically transmitted in most cases. Tourette's is one of a number of conditions classified as tic disorders. It has several forms, one of which is manifested in *complex phonic tics*. These represent involuntary utterances or expressions, such as repetitive phrases, animal sounds, unusual changes in voice pitch or volume, stuttering, and coprolalia (use of socially taboo phrases or obscenities).

PSYCHOLOGICAL The release of nervous tension or a nervous habit may account for inappropriate noises or comments. In some cases, this behavior may be secondarily reinforced by social reactions.

SOCIAL Some students tend to receive social recognition for silliness, which may involve inappropriate sounds or comments.

Because these behaviors are reinforced by peers' laughter or other reactions, the student chooses social status in spite of negative classroom consequences.

What to Do

- Speak with the student privately and find out whether the utterances are voluntary or involuntary.

- If the utterances appear to be involuntary, consult with the parents and see whether the student needs to be checked for neurological or medical problems.

- If you ascertain that the inappropriate utterances are voluntary, explain to the student that you will not tolerate this type of behavior in your classroom.

- If the inappropriate behavior stops, reward the student privately. Let her know that you are aware of her efforts to control her behavior.

- If the behavior does not stop, administer appropriate consequences (see the steps subsequently described).

- In order to deal with this pattern, you must understand that the student's need for attention is not the problem. The problem is the student's choice of behaviors to derive attention. Therefore, you need to take the following steps:

  1. Give the student controlled attention when she least expects it. For example, go to her or call her to your desk for reassurance or observation of a positive behavior. Let the student know at the end of the day the behaviors that you found most positive.

  2. Meet with the student privately and preempt the inappropriate behavior. Tell the student before she enters the classroom that you will not tolerate inappropriate noises or comments and that there will be serious consequences if the comments persist. (You should determine the consequences beforehand.) Explain that you expect cooperation and that, if necessary, you will provide the student with other outlets for her expressions. You may need to repeat this procedure several times to reinforce your seriousness.

3. When the student raises her hand, provide verbal praise to reinforce this appropriate behavior.

4. Seat the student next to a peer who exhibits behaviors that you would like reinforced.

5. Do not reinforce the inappropriate behavior by laughing at the student's comments or noises, even if they are amusing. Your reaction will only aggravate the situation.

- If necessary, consult with the school counseling or social work staff, the school psychologist, or the pupil personnel team.

Competitiveness

ACADEMIC   Academics create a sense of competition in many students. Many students know that being in the top 10 or 20 percent of the class affects their ability to get into college and their future job opportunities. Competitiveness often accompanies this knowledge.

ENVIRONMENTAL   Adolescents with parents who push very hard may become competitive because they feel that doing so is the only way to get parental approval. In addition, adolescents who have older siblings who have excelled in certain areas may become competitive because they wish to match or exceed their siblings' performance.

INTELLECTUAL   Adolescents with high intelligence often know they have great potential to succeed academically. Because they know they have the ability to excel, they tend to compete to do so.

PSYCHOLOGICAL   Numerous psychological reasons exist for an adolescent's competitiveness: perfectionism, obsessive-compulsive tendencies, and low self-esteem among them. Generally, being very competitive suggests some degree of insecurity. Feeling the need to be better than everyone else also may be a sign of hidden frustration and anxiety.

SOCIAL   Adolescents often compete with one another, as individuals and as groups. High group performance (e.g., being the winning team) can create a sense of group cohesion. Individual excellence may increase social status. Excessive competition in groups or individually, however, can result in disharmony and other social problems.

What to Do

- Competition is to a certain degree healthy and normal. It is only unhealthy when it becomes excessive. If you see that an adolescent is being overly competitive, talk privately with him about his need to be this way. Discuss his motivations and the possible negative consequences of excessive competitiveness.

- Confer with parents to determine the possible role of family expectations and to enlist their help in giving the adolescent permission to "slow down."

- If the problem persists or interferes with the adolescent's functioning, consult with the school counseling or social work staff, the school psychologist, or the pupil personnel team.

Difficulty Grasping Concepts

Why Students
May Exhibit This Behavior

ACADEMIC   Everyone finds certain concepts inherently easier to grasp than others. Moreover, a student may be strong in certain areas and weaker in other areas. These are facts of academic life.

ENVIRONMENTAL   Some adolescents have parents whose own education was cut short. These parents may be limited in the assistance they can give with homework. Without parental coaching, these students may fall behind and have trouble mastering progressively difficult concepts.

INTELLECTUAL   One aspect of intelligence is the ability to learn. The higher one's intelligence, the greater one's capacity to learn new concepts. If a student has low intelligence, he will have difficulty understanding and grasping new concepts that other students may find easy. Additionally, students with higher intelligence more readily grasp abstract concepts. Because their thinking tends to be more concrete, students with lower intelligence have more difficulty with abstract concepts.

LINGUISTIC   A student who has problems understanding language will also have great difficulty grasping certain concepts if they are either delivered too quickly or delivered in language he cannot understand (for instance, if the language of instruction is not the student's first language).

PERCEPTUAL   Grasping certain concepts can be very difficult for a student who has perceptual problems. One of the classic examples concerns learning certain movements in gym class. When students square dance, they follow certain rules for moving left, right, and so on. For students with perceptual problems, this can become increasingly difficult (for some it is impossible without proper training) and ultimately can lead to failure.

PSYCHOLOGICAL   A student may resist grasping concepts in an attempt to gain attention. If the teacher immediately responds to the student's request for help rather than giving him time to grasp a concept on his own, the student realizes that claiming not to understand is a way to be recognized and showered with extra time. Alternatively, a student who has difficulty grasping concepts may be suffering from anxiety, which greatly limits his capacity to concentrate, memorize, and focus.

SOCIAL   Some students may not grasp concepts because they may be preoccupied with their friends. Also, they may not want to admit that they understand certain concepts if most of their peers do not.

What to Do

- Speak privately with the student. Ask him which areas are giving him the most problems and why he thinks the problems are occurring.

- Assure the student that it is all right to tell the truth. This way, if the source of the difficulty is your teaching style, he will not be afraid to identify what is truly problematic for him.

- Assure the student that you are not punishing him but rather that you are trying to help. He needs to feel comfortable talking with you because he may be embarrassed about the situation.

- If you feel that the student's difficulties are the result of feeling overwhelmed, being anxious, or fearing failure, you may want to present him with shorter but more frequent exercises. It is possible that the student has the ability to grasp the concept but that anxiety clouds his thinking and thus limits his performance. A student who is very anxious needs to feel empowered and more in control in order to move forward academically. A series of success experiences over time can confer this sense of control. After identifying the concept that is problematic for the student, tell him that you will not call on him in class when this topic arises unless he raises his hand. This will allay his anxiety.

- Offer to meet with the student before, during, or after school to help him with the concepts that are difficult.

- If appropriate, consult with the school counseling or social work staff, the school psychologist, or the pupil personnel team.

Controlling Behavior

Why Students
May Exhibit This Behavior

ACADEMIC   Students who do poorly in school may be very controlling as they attempt to regain status that they lose through academic failure.

ENVIRONMENTAL   Some adolescents who are controlling have parents who set few boundaries or who pave every road so that the adolescent does not become frustrated. Such parents usually lack confidence in their parenting abilities, so they give the adolescent everything and demand nothing. In such a case, the adolescent leads the parents and faces the world without a sense of protection. Because the parents are not offering a buffer against the outside world, the adolescent, out of panic, seeks to control to ward off something unknown but feared. Other adolescents may be controlling because they themselves are overly controlled at home. Students who experience very tight boundaries, rigid parenting, overreaction, and so on may copy this or take it out on other students. A sense of control over others may make them feel less victimized.

INTELLECTUAL   See *Academic*.

LINGUISTIC   See *Academic*.

MEDICAL   A student with medical concerns may be controlling in reaction to fear and an inability to control her medical situation.

PERCEPTUAL   A student with perceptual deficits may be controlling because of an inability to process information in a way that would allow her to maintain a proper perspective. Often, she may misread a situation, misinterpret another student's actions or gestures, or be unaware of social subtleties.

PSYCHOLOGICAL   A student who always needs to be in control may be responding out of intense fear, panic, or anxiety. The more controlling a student is, the more out of control she actually feels. She is trying to make her life predictable and manageable, not realizing that one needs to be flexible to survive. When people or situations do not conform to the student's need to control, she enters a panic state, which may be characterized by tantrums, cursing, yelling, and so on.

SOCIAL Controlling behavior may be an attempt to be noticed by others. A student who feels socially insignificant may think that controlling others will provide her with a social audience. However, many students will soon reject her because she is so controlling. Rejection in turn will make her more anxious and increase her need to control.

What to Do

- We suggest a three-part approach for dealing with controlling behavior:

  1. Speak privately with the student and set boundaries around the controlling behavior. Keeping in mind that the need to control is a sign not of strength but rather of a fragile ego, do not hesitate to establish yourself as the benevolent authority. Explain that, although you know the student may have issues underlying her behavior and that you will help her try to understand them, you will not tolerate the behavior. Convey predetermined consequences for continued inappropriate behavior.

  2. Help the student understand why she is being controlling. Ask her to verbalize what she is feeling or why she does what she does. If she is unable to verbalize her feelings, you may want to provide her with some labels. For example, you might say that you have seen other students who needed to control because they felt they were not doing well in school, had problems at home, or felt rejected by other students.

  3. Consult with the school counseling or social work staff or the school psychologist about the possibility of setting up a meeting with the parents or developing a behavioral contract for the student.

- If the problem is severe and persists, consult the school's pupil personnel team.

Inability to Handle Criticism

Why Students
May Exhibit This Behavior

ACADEMIC   Some adolescents believe that they are always right where schoolwork is concerned and, because of their academic success, feel as though they are right in everything. When offered constructive criticism, they can become extremely defensive. Others may have had negative experiences with teachers whom they may have perceived as too critical. These adolescents are very afraid of academic criticism because they cannot take it constructively.

ENVIRONMENTAL   At home, some adolescents hear only negative words and criticism. Consequently, they become extremely self-protective. When they receive constructive criticism about schoolwork, they immediately put up barriers.

INTELLECTUAL   Students with limited intelligence may not be able to do things as fast or as well as their peers. They may become very sensitive to criticism because of their inability to succeed.

LINGUISTIC   Students who feel insecure about their expressive language ability may become very defensive and lose perspective when they receive constructive criticism aimed at improving their language skills.

PERCEPTUAL   See *Linguistic*.

PSYCHOLOGICAL   Students who have low self-esteem and fragile egos commonly distort what is being said. They can be very sensitive and take everything personally. When such students receive constructive criticism they often take it quite hard, believing that criticism reflects on them as people rather than on specific aspects of their work.

SOCIAL   If adolescents receive constructive criticism in front of peers, they may react very defensively, fearing teasing or ridicule.

Because of their social need for acceptance, they react to the criticism in a very negative manner.

What to Do

- Speak privately with the student to discuss how he is doing and how he feels about himself. Explain the purpose of constructive criticism and assure him that your criticism is not aimed at him or his ability.

- Discuss with the student how you hope to make him feel better through successful experiences that will help him see himself as capable and adequate.

- Give the student tasks at which you know he can excel. In the process, boost the student's academic self-confidence so that he is motivated toward future learning. Because confidence is a result of repeated successful experiences, you may want to begin with tasks that ensure 100 percent success: shorter but more frequent assignments; less demanding problems; alternative means of responding, such as audiotapes or charts; a daily progress report that focuses on the positives; and classroom duties that place the student in a positive light with his classmates, such as collecting or handing out papers or leading the class in some activity.

- If necessary, consult with the school counseling or social work staff or the school psychologist about the possibility of including the student in a self-esteem group.

- If the problem is severe and persists, consult with the school's pupil personnel team.

Criticism of Others

ACADEMIC   Students who feel insecure about their academic weaknesses may attempt to devalue those more competent through criticism.

ENVIRONMENTAL   The old saying "We live what we learn" may be applicable here, especially if the adolescent is exposed to a great deal of criticism at home. The adolescent may look for someone at school to victimize as he is victimized at home. In other cases, students may criticize others to vent extreme tension and frustration generated by home problems. Such misdirected criticism is usually impulsive and delivered without awareness of consequences.

INTELLECTUAL   A student with limited intellectual abilities may be critical of others in an attempt to elevate his own status, which he feels is very low.

LINGUISTIC   See *Academic.*

PERCEPTUAL   A student with perceptual difficulties may misperceive or misread the actions of others. He may consequently feel threatened and become critical as a defense against what he believes he perceives.

PSYCHOLOGICAL   A student who feels very vulnerable or inadequate may resort to criticism as a method of getting people to back off. He will do this out of fear that another person will learn too much about him or see the faults that he sees in himself.

SOCIAL   Some students may resort to criticism in attempts to lower the social status of others who are more popular. Other students may become critical of people they feel are not paying attention to them.

What to Do

- Speak privately with the student and discuss what you have observed about his behavior. Ask the student his opinion of the behavior.

- Determine whether or not the student realizes what he is doing. Some students have a thin layer of denial and, when confronted, will own up to their behavior. However, other students have thick layers of denial. If that appears to be the case, tread lightly and consult the school counseling or social work staff or the school psychologist.

- Assuming that the student understands what he is doing but is not sure how to change it, explain to him why his behavior is detrimental to his making friends and succeeding in school.

- Try to offer the student ideas, options, and alternatives for what to do when he feels the need to criticize others. For instance, seat him closer to you so that he may feel more secure and connected. Tell him that, if he needs to criticize others, he may want to come to you first and discuss his motives.

- Try to discern patterns in the occurrence of this behavior. There may be a theme underlying the issues, experiences, or situations because criticizing others is an attempt to refocus the spotlight, especially in situations where the student feels inadequate.

- Praise the student when he refrains from criticism and instead uses some other method to solve a problem.

- If the situation persists, confer with the parents about possible underlying circumstances.

- If necessary, consult the school counseling or social work staff, the school psychologist, or the pupil personnel team.

Criticism of Self

Why Students
May Exhibit This Behavior

ACADEMIC   Consistent academic failure may frustrate a student so much that she becomes self-critical to the point of functional impairment. Some students may exhibit this behavior briefly out of frustration or disgust if they fail tests, forget assignments, and so on. The issue here is always the intensity and frequency of the behavior.

ENVIRONMENTAL   Some adolescents may be self-critical because they have highly demanding or critical parents. They are either reflecting what they believe their parents feel about them or expressing anger at themselves for being unable to please their parents. Some adolescents may be critical of themselves because they feel they cannot live up to parental expectations. Still others may be comparing themselves with high-achieving siblings.

INTELLECTUAL   Low intellectual ability resulting in continuous frustration and failure may lead the student to consider herself inadequate and become self-critical.

LINGUISTIC   See *Perceptual.*

PERCEPTUAL   A student who experiences perceptual frustration in spite of intellectual ability can react by taking out certain feelings on herself. All frustration, if unrelieved, eventually turns to anger, which in this case is directed inward.

PSYCHOLOGICAL   Students may make derogatory statements about themselves for several reasons. Some students are seeking reassurance or attention. Some students may truly believe their statements and may be communicating intense frustration and crying out for help. Others may, out of low self-esteem, use such statements in an effort to soften fear of the failure that they expect to experience. Still other students may use this behavior

as a means of gaining sympathy and attention, especially if surrounded by individuals who tend to enable or rescue.

SOCIAL   Consistent social rejection, embarrassment, victimization, or isolation may lead a student to make derogatory statements about herself. Her feelings of social worthlessness may be
too difficult to tolerate. In some cases, students may resort to
this behavior to gain social attention, albeit negative. Any spotlight is better than none.

What to Do

- Speak privately with the student to discuss how she is doing
  and how she feels about herself.

- Give the student tasks at which you know she can excel. In
  the process, boost the student's academic self-confidence so
  that she is motivated toward future learning. Because confidence is a result of repeated successful experiences, you may
  want to begin with tasks that ensure 100 percent success:
  shorter but more frequent assignments; less demanding
  problems; alternative means of responding, such as audiotapes or charts; a daily progress report that focuses on the
  positives; and classroom duties that place the student in a
  positive light with her classmates, such as collecting or
  handing out papers or leading the class in some activity.

- Give the student all possible forms of positive reinforcement.
  Get ideas from the school psychologist or other teachers.

- If necessary, consult with the school counseling or social
  work staff or the school psychologist about the possibility of
  including the student in a self-esteem group.

- If the problem is severe and persists, consult with the
  school's pupil personnel team.

Crying

Why Students
May Exhibit This Behavior

ACADEMIC   For some adolescents, the ultimate proof of self-worth lies in academic grades. When they succeed at school they are good kids, and when they do poorly they are bad kids. Given the personal value grades play in these adolescents' lives, when they fail in school, they cannot deal with the resulting emotional devastation and react by crying.

ENVIRONMENTAL   Some adolescents live in homes where crying is the norm. They observe crying family members immediately comforted by all those around them. Adolescents can emulate this behavior and learn that crying can also bring them attention, even if prompted by minor upsets. Other adolescents may cry in response to stressors at home such as separation, continuous arguing, or violence.

INTELLECTUAL   See *Linguistic, Perceptual,* and *Psychological.*

LINGUISTIC   An inability to express oneself can be tremendously frustrating for children. A student who is hurting may not be able to put this feeling into words and may then give in to the natural human impulse to cry.

MEDICAL   Some students may be physically sensitive or medically fragile, experiencing atypical physical pain if they are softly bumped or hit. This hypersensitivity can lead to immediate crying.

PERCEPTUAL   Students with perceptual problems know the daily frustration of not seeing the world as everyone else does. Eventually, their frustrations build to the point where crying is the natural outlet.

PSYCHOLOGICAL   Students may be hypersensitive and cry for various reasons. Some may have low self-esteem and take what others say much too personally. Others cannot verbalize their true feelings, so the only way they know to respond or to release tension is to do what comes naturally—cry.

SOCIAL   Some adolescents may cry easily because they do not fit in social situations but do not really know why. They express the resulting hurt and frustration by crying.

What to Do

- Try to determine whether the student cries for legitimate reasons or is simply hypersensitive. Help the student understand why she cries so easily and how to respond to situations without crying.

- If the child cannot explain why she cries easily, help her to verbalize her feelings by being patient and reassuring. You may also want to provide labels for any emotions you think the student may be feeling.

- If the student is very sensitive, encourage her to share with you any problems she may be having before the crying begins.

- When speaking with a student who cries easily, use a soft and reassuring tone because she may withdraw quickly if she feels threatened.

- Have the student work in groups with classmates who tend to be in tune with the feelings of others.

- Confer with the parents to determine whether there are underlying problems of which you are not aware.

- If necessary, consult with the school counseling or social work staff or the school psychologist about the possibility of including the student in a self-esteem group.

- If the problem is severe and persists, consult with the school's pupil personnel team.

Cursing

Why Students
May Exhibit This Behavior

ACADEMIC   Some adolescents curse because of their poor academic performance. Their inability to succeed in school becomes overwhelming, and they displace their anger at others through the use of inappropriate verbal expressions.

ENVIRONMENTAL   Unfortunately, some adolescents curse as a result of the behaviors they see modeled by parents and other family members. This is a familiar response that tends to be repeated.

INTELLECTUAL   Intelligence involves many verbal qualities. Those with below-average intelligence may not know how to release their needs and wants in a socially appropriate manner. In addition, if they are frustrated, they may release this feeling through cursing.

LINGUISTIC   Adolescents with language difficulties or for whom the language of instruction is not the native language may be quite frustrated at school. They become upset, do not know how to deal with the tension, and resort to cursing to express their feelings.

MEDICAL   In the rare case, an adolescent who has Tourette's syndrome may curse involuntarily.

PERCEPTUAL   Perceptual problems can lead to frustration in all areas of life. The only way some adolescents know to release frustration is to curse.

PSYCHOLOGICAL   Psychological problems may cause some adolescents to become very hostile and aggressive. Because they have "short fuses," they may scream at others when something bothers them. Their choice of language will often be cursing.

SOCIAL   Cursing is a social thing to do. If an adolescent hears his buddies cursing, he will likely feel under pressure to use the same kind of language. Even if he knows cursing is unacceptable and unnecessary, avoiding it may make him feel uncomfortable and alienate him from the group.

What to Do

- Meet privately with the adolescent and explain what is and is not appropriate classroom language. Discuss the adolescent's impact on others and explain how his behavior is creating problems for himself and others. Explain the consequences if the cursing continues. (These should be predetermined.)

- Help the adolescent verbalize his feelings. He may be having difficulty verbalizing what he is feeling and act out resultant frustration by cursing. Provide appropriate labels for what the adolescent is feeling.

- Be sure not to put the adolescent down in front of his classmates. This will embarrass him and perhaps even make him angrier.

- Discuss with the counseling or social work staff or the school psychologist whether there are underlying familial or emotional problems.

- If the problem is severe and persists, bring the situation to the attention of the pupil personnel team.

Daydreaming

Why Students
May Exhibit This Behavior

ACADEMIC Some students daydream in school simply because they are bored with the subject matter. Adolescents have a tremendous potential to tune out what they do not like. When they tune out, they will begin to daydream about sports, social activities, and many other past or future events.

ENVIRONMENTAL Some adolescents have home lives fraught with constant conflict, fear, anxiety, and tension. In reaction, they will often go into their own worlds and fantasize about living in better homes or situations.

PSYCHOLOGICAL Daydreaming may be prompted by deep-rooted psychological issues. It can be a serious way to escape from the real world. In some students, low self-esteem and inability to understand why certain things are the way they are create sadness and discontent. Daydreaming becomes the only way they can cope in a world that they believe is unfair and not right for them.

SOCIAL For some students, daydreaming is stimulated by social events—for instance, an upcoming school dance, party, or sports event. In their minds they may be choosing dance partners or hitting home runs.

What to Do

- Keep in mind that daydreaming should be a concern only if a pattern exists and the frequency and duration are problematic. The fact is that everyone daydreams at some time.
- Check with the school nurse and the student's parents to be sure that there is no medical problem that may be causing the student to daydream.

- Try to ascertain if a pattern exists in the student's daydreaming. See if it occurs more frequently in the morning, a possible sign of exhaustion, or in the afternoon, a sign of possible fatigue from a long school day. Note during which subjects the student daydreams.
- Ask the student why she feels that she daydreams.
- Reinforce the student with verbal praise when you notice her on task, however briefly. This will help build her confidence.
- When the student needs to stay on task, get involved with what she is doing. By interacting with her, you may improve her chances of focusing.
- Have the student work in groups with classmates who you know have very good attention spans.
- Change the topics in the lesson as often as possible. Get ideas from other teachers.
- Seat the student in the front of the class to improve her chances of attending to the subject matter.
- Without making it too obvious, call on the student more often than on others. Keeping her on her toes will increase her chances of staying focused.
- If the problem is severe and persists, consult with the school counseling or social work staff, the school psychologist, or the pupil personnel team.

Defying Authority

Why Students
May Exhibit This Behavior

ACADEMIC   Students with histories of failure and academic insecurity may lash out at those they perceive created their problems. Anger directed at school authorities may be displaced feelings of inadequacy and frustration.

ENVIRONMENTAL   Adolescents from homes where certain parenting styles are evident may lack experience with authority, boundaries, consistent rules, and consequences. Without such experience, an adolescent never incorporates the internal parent that guides conscience and internalizes rules of society. The adolescent may consequently lack respect for authority and instead be guided by his own rules, which often get him into trouble. In other cases, adolescents who come from violent or abusive homes may defy authority in expressions of displaced anger.

INTELLECTUAL   Students with limited intellectual ability may not grasp the relationship between actions and consequences or recognize levels of authority. As a result, they react to all authority in the same manner.

PSYCHOLOGICAL   In a milder form, defiance of authority may be exhibited by students who are so anxious that they are not fully aware of their behavior, its consequences, and the levels of authority involved. In more severe forms, defiance of authority can be symptomatic of oppositional defiant disorder or conduct disorder.

- Oppositional defiant disorder, the less serious of the two, is usually characterized by patterns of negative, hostile, and defiant behaviors with peers and adults. These behaviors may include swearing and frequent episodes of intense anger and annoyance. The behaviors associated with oppositional defiant disorder usually appear around age 8, generally not later than early adolescence. In the classroom, students with this disorder may exhibit low frustration tolerance, frequent temper outbursts, low self-confidence, unwillingness to take responsibility for their actions, and consistent blaming of others for their own mistakes or problems.

- Conduct disorder is characterized by a persistent pattern of intrusive behavior that violates the basic rights of others and shows no concern for implications or consequences. This pattern is not selective and is exhibited in the home, at school, with the student's peers, and in the community. This condition may also manifest itself in vandalism, stealing, physical aggression, cruelty to animals, or fire setting. In school, conduct-disordered students may be physically confrontational with teachers and peers, have poor attendance, and exhibit other forms of antisocial behavior. Moreover, they may frequently be suspended, thereby missing a great deal of academic work.

SOCIAL   Students who defy authority may be succumbing to peer pressure or the strong need to be accepted by a group or gang that prides itself on antisocial behavior and defiance of authority.

What to Do

- We recommend a three-step approach for dealing with defiant behavior:

  1. Set boundaries around the inappropriate behavior. Speak privately with the student and, keeping in mind that defiance of authority is a sign not of strength but of a fragile ego, establish yourself as the benevolent authority. Explain that although you understand that the student may have underlying issues and that you will help him try to understand them, you will not tolerate the inappropriate behavior. Stress the seriousness of the situation and the consequences if it persists.

  2. Try to help the student understand why he is defiant. Encourage him to verbalize what he is feeling or why he does what he does. If he cannot give voice to his feelings, you may want to provide him with some labels. For

example, you may want to say that you have seen other students defy authority because they felt they were not doing well in school, had problems at home, or felt rejected by peers.

3. If the defiant behavior follows a consistent pattern, confer with the student's parents to obtain information about any issues at home.

- Consult with the school counseling or social work staff or the school psychologist about developing a behavioral contract for the student. Parent involvement will be important.

- If the problem is severe and persists, consult the school's pupil personnel team.

Depression

Why Students
May Exhibit This Behavior

ACADEMIC   Years of academic struggle and failure can adversely affect a student's self-esteem and generate a feeling of hopelessness. This pattern may result in some forms of depression.

ENVIRONMENTAL   Family patterns of depression, extreme and prolonged stress, illness, constant fighting, and severe economic pressure affecting the family structure may all contribute to feelings of hopelessness and depression in some adolescents.

LINGUISTIC   Inability to express themselves can be tremendously frustrating for adolescents. When they become upset and cannot put their hurt into words, depression may be the result.

MEDICAL   Depression may result from a biochemical imbalance.

PERCEPTUAL   Students with perceptual problems do not see the world as everyone else does. The daily frustration this causes may eventually be turned inward, causing depression.

PSYCHOLOGICAL   There are many psychological triggers that may result in depression. The key is to recognize the signs. These may include poor appetite, difficulty sleeping, low energy, general fatigue, low self-esteem, difficulty concentrating, and feelings of hopelessness. A pattern of depressed mood is always cause for concern.

SOCIAL   Some students may experience depression arising from social isolation, rejection, intimidation, or victimization over a period of time. This depression may stem from a diminished sense of social worth and a lack of social connection.

What to Do

Depression in young people is a very serious and often complex issue and can take many forms. Therefore, we strongly recommend that if you suspect that a student is depressed, immediately consult with the school psychologist and the principal for reasons of the student's safety, your and the school's liability, and the parents' rights. It is important not to take any chances.

Destroying Own Work

Why Students
May Exhibit This Behavior

ACADEMIC   Students with low academic self-confidence may be extremely critical of their work to the point that destroying it is a way to avoid confronting another potential failure. A student may start out with a desire to do the assignment. However, the tension from not understanding it, having trouble completing it, or believing that it will be criticized may trigger this behavior pattern.

ENVIRONMENTAL   Adolescents with overly critical parents may destroy their work in an expression of displaced anger. Other adolescents may resort to this behavior to avoid anticipated parental criticism.

INTELLECTUAL   Students with limited intellectual ability may destroy their work because its poor quality causes great frustration and embarrassment.

LINGUISTIC   Students who have trouble understanding the language, either because they have individual limitations or because the language of instruction is not their first language, may destroy their work out of frustration.

PERCEPTUAL   See *Academic.*

PSYCHOLOGICAL   Students with low self-esteem tend to have distorted perceptions and to see things more negatively than reality justifies. Moreover, such students, in their emotional fragility, have difficulty tolerating criticism. They may destroy their work to avoid facing critical comments or suggestions. Other students are perfectionists and may resort to this action because nothing they do satisfies them.

SOCIAL   Fear of ridicule and embarrassment may force a student to destroy her work.

What to Do

- Speak privately with the student. Keeping in mind that destroying one's work indicates feelings of inadequacy, discuss the seriousness of the situation and the consequences for the student's self-esteem and reputation with peers if the behavior continues. Remember that no student wants to fail. This student may lack the skills or understanding to cope with her issues and needs not criticism but reassurance and nurturing.

- Encourage the student to verbalize what she is feeling or why she does what she does. If she cannot give voice to her feelings, you may want to provide some labels for what she may be feeling.

- Suggest to the student alternative means of dealing with her frustration. Many students who consistently destroy their work do not know appropriate ways to handle difficult and stressful situations.

- If destruction of work is a consistent pattern, confer with the student's parents.

- Consult with the school counseling or social work staff or the school psychologist about developing a behavioral contract for the student.

- If the problem is severe and persists, consult with the school's pupil personnel team.

Destroying Others' Property

Why Students
May Exhibit This Behavior

ACADEMIC   Displaced frustration resulting from academic insecurity or failure may cause students to act out toward those whom they perceive as more capable.

ENVIRONMENTAL   The act of destroying another's property may be a release of tension stemming from extreme instability or dysfunction at home. In this case, it is not a well-thought-out act but a misguided displacement of emotions. In other cases, this behavior may emulate what is learned or modeled at home—for instance, if the student's own possessions are destroyed or taken away.

INTELLECTUAL   See *Academic.*

PSYCHOLOGICAL   Although in most cases destruction of another's property is an isolated incident, it may be a sign of a deeper disturbance, such as conduct disorder or oppositional defiant disorder, which may require more professional intervention. In such cases, the overreactions can be intense, violent, and consistent, and may be directed toward both peers and authority figures.

- Oppositional defiant disorder, the less serious of the two, is usually characterized by patterns of negative, hostile, and defiant behaviors with peers and adults. These behaviors may include swearing and frequent episodes of intense anger and annoyance. The behaviors associated with oppositional defiant disorder usually appear around age 8, generally not later than early adolescence. In the classroom, students with this disorder may exhibit low frustration tolerance, frequent temper outbursts, low self-confidence, unwillingness to take responsibility for their actions, and consistent blaming of others for their own mistakes or problems.

- Conduct disorder is characterized by a persistent pattern of intrusive behavior that violates the basic rights of others and shows no concern for implications or consequences. This pattern is not selective and is exhibited in the home, at school, with the student's peers, and in the community. This condition may also manifest itself in vandalism, stealing, physical aggression, cruelty to animals, or fire setting. In school, conduct-disordered students may be physically confrontational with teachers and peers, have poor attendance, and exhibit other forms of antisocial behavior. Moreover, they may frequently be suspended, thereby missing a great deal of academic work.

SOCIAL   Social rejection and a desire for retaliation may underlie the destruction of the property of others.

What to Do

- We recommend a three-part approach for dealing with this problem:

  1. Set boundaries around the inappropriate behavior. Speak privately with the student. Keeping in mind that the destruction of others' property is a sign not of strength but of a fragile ego, establish yourself as the benevolent authority. Explain that although you realize that the student may have issues that give rise to his behavior and you will help him try to understand them, you will not tolerate the behavior. Reinforce the seriousness of the situation and the consequences if it persists.

  2. Try to help the student understand why he is destroying others' property. Encourage him to verbalize what he is feeling and why he does what he does. If he cannot give voice to his feelings, you may want to provide some labels for what he may be feeling. For example, you may want to say that you have seen other students destroying property because they felt they were not doing well in school, had problems at home, or felt rejected by others.

  3. Help the student change his behavior pattern. Suggest alternative means of dealing with stress and frustration. Many students who destroy things do not know appropriate ways to handle difficult situations. In addition, make sure that the student apologizes to the person whose property he destroyed. This will help him develop a sense of responsibility for his behavior.

- If destruction of property is a consistent pattern, confer with the student's parents.
- Consult with the school counseling or social work staff or the school psychologist about developing a behavioral contract for the student.
- If the problem is severe and persists, consult with the school's pupil personnel team.

Inability to Follow
Verbal Directions

Why Students
May Exhibit This Behavior

ACADEMIC   Fear of failing or being unable to understand concepts may cause a student to resist understanding directions in a rationalization for not doing something. Further, some students do not understand what words mean or how to interpret directions. Their underlying deficiencies in decoding skills, reading rate, and reading comprehension may cause problems with following directions in all areas of life.

ENVIRONMENTAL   Some adolescents who have overly critical, dysfunctional, or abusive families may develop high levels of tension, which can impair their ability to concentrate and remember. Others lack structure and control at home and are unaccustomed to following directions because they experience no consequences for not doing so.

INTELLECTUAL   Students with limited intellectual ability usually have secondary difficulties with memory, retention, comprehension, or language. All these factors may compromise a student's ability to understand directions, especially those that involve several steps.

LINGUISTIC   Certain types of receptive language disorders may make it difficult for students to understand, comprehend, retain, and follow directions. Also, a student who has difficulty with language comprehension inevitably will have great difficulty following directions.

MEDICAL   Certain medications can impair a student's ability to remember things or concentrate. Some students may have neurological conditions that create processing problems with respect to understanding and following directions. Also, hearing difficulties may be at the root of this pattern.

PERCEPTUAL Certain types of perceptual deficits, especially those affecting memory and auditory perception, may greatly interfere with a student's ability to understand and remember directions. Further, if a student perceives things from a different perspective than others or hears but cannot sort out what is being said, understanding and following directions will be extremely difficult.

PSYCHOLOGICAL In some students, high anxiety can interfere directly with memory: As anxiety goes up, memory and concentration go down, and the ability to retain and follow directions may be impaired. In others, failure to follow directions stems from simple defiance and opposition to authority.

SOCIAL Often, succumbing to peer pressure, a student will not follow directions because no one else is following them. She may know this is wrong but may follow the pack simply because she is afraid to go against the norm.

What to Do

- Confer with the adolescent's parents or the school nurse to determine whether the adolescent's hearing needs to be checked.

- Ask the speech/language therapist to screen the student. It is possible that even though the student's hearing is fine, he may have language or auditory processing problems.

- Determine whether other students seem to be having similar problems understanding directions. If that is the case, review your directions and consider simplifying them or breaking them down into smaller components.

- Consult with the school psychologist to determine whether any circumstances in the student's life might be creating tension, which could undercut memory and concentration and cause difficulty with directions.

- If underlying problems are ruled out and it can be assumed that the student has the ability to follow directions, try the following techniques:

  1. Talk with the student and elicit her perception of what is going on.

2. Ask the student what is causing her the greatest difficulty and whether she can suggest ways for you to help.

3. Avoid complex directions.

4. Give the student written directions along with verbal directions.

5. Determine whether or not the student's inability to follow directions stems from an attitudinal problem. If you believe this to be the case, establish reinforcers and penalties for following or not following directions. If the student follows through, compliment and reward her. If she does not, administer an appropriate and fair punishment.

- If necessary, consult with the school counseling or social work staff or the school psychologist about the possibility of setting up a behavior modification program for the student.
- If the problem is severe and persists, consult with the school's pupil personnel team.

Inability to Follow Written Directions

Why Students
May Exhibit This Behavior

ACADEMIC Students who lack reading comprehension or decoding skills obviously may have trouble understanding written directions.

INTELLECTUAL Students with limited intellectual ability often find written directions confusing, overwhelming, or too complicated.

LINGUISTIC Students with language disabilities or those for whom the language of instruction is not the first language often have great difficulties with written assignments. For instance, a bilingual student may read directions in English, think in his first language, and revert back to English to respond.

MEDICAL Poor vision may compromise a student's ability to understand written directions.

PERCEPTUAL Some students with visual perceptual problems may have difficulty understanding and responding to written directions of any complexity because processes such as internal organization, memory, and so on may be impaired.

PSYCHOLOGICAL Some states of tension can result in a pattern of withholding known as passive resistance, sometimes manifested in an unconscious need not to follow any form of directions issued by an authority figure.

What to Do

- Confer with the adolescent's parents or the school nurse to determine whether the adolescent's vision needs to be checked.

- Ask the professional on your staff responsible for educational evaluations to screen the student. It is possible that even though the student's vision is fine, he may have visual processing problems.

- Determine whether other students seem to be having similar problems understanding directions. If that is the case, review your written directions and consider simplifying them or breaking them down into smaller components.

- Consult with the school psychologist to determine whether any circumstances in the student's life might be creating tension, which could undercut memory and concentration and cause difficulty with directions.

- If underlying problems are ruled out and it can be assumed that the student has the ability to follow directions, try these techniques:

  1. Talk with the student and elicit his perception of what is going on.
  2. Ask the student what is causing him the greatest difficulty and whether he can suggest ways for you to help.
  3. Avoid complex written directions.
  4. Accompany written directions with verbal directions.
  5. Determine whether or not the student's inability to follow directions stems from an attitudinal problem. If you believe this to be the case, establish reinforcers and penalties for following or not following directions. If the student follows through, compliment and reward him. If he does not, administer an appropriate and fair punishment.

- If necessary, consult with the school counseling or social work staff or the school psychologist about the possibility of setting up a behavior modification program for the student.

- If the problem is severe and persists, consult with the school's pupil personnel team.

Distractibility

Why Students
May Exhibit This Behavior

ACADEMIC Some students have great difficulty focusing on more than one academic task. Given more than one thing to do, they will often become quite distracted. When academic demands are not fully structured, they cannot stay on task.

ENVIRONMENTAL Some adolescents are distractible because they are surrounded by too many stimuli at home. For example, if the TV is on, siblings are fighting, Mom is on the phone, and Dad is calling the adolescent, she will be unable to concentrate on homework. For some students, distractibility may be a symptom of preoccupation with family issues such as parental conflict, financial problems, alcohol abuse, or violence.

INTELLECTUAL See *Psychological*.

LINGUISTIC See *Psychological*.

MEDICAL Students with attention deficit/hyperactivity disorder (AD/HD) will be distractible and easily influenced by extraneous stimuli. These students often have great difficulty focusing on tasks and following through on directions.

PERCEPTUAL See *Psychological*.

PSYCHOLOGICAL Psychological reasons for distractibility are numerous. Increased tension, preoccupation, low self-esteem, feelings of inadequacy, and depression are just a few.

SOCIAL Although in many life events there are two or more activities occurring simultaneously, some students cannot handle more than one thing at a time. Complex social stimulation causes them to be unable to focus on tasks at hand.

What to Do

- Check with the school nurse and the student's parents to rule out medical problems that might be causing distractibility.

- Try to limit auditory and visual stimuli in the classroom so that the student does not have too many things to focus on at one time.

- Ask the student why she feels that she is distractible and what may be contributing to her distractibility.

- Give verbal praise when you notice the student on task, however briefly. This will help build her confidence.

- Try to get involved with the student's activities when she needs to stay on task. Your interaction may increase her focus.

- Have the student work in groups with classmates who you know have very good attention spans.

- Have the student write down what it is exactly that she must do. Often students who cannot stay on task will forget directions because they have been focusing on other stimuli. Having the directions written down enables the student to get back on track and maintain her original focus.

- Try to change the topics in the lesson as often as possible. This may be difficult if you have a large number of students in your class. Find out how other teachers handle this situation.

- Seat the student in the front of the room to minimize her chances of being distracted by other stimuli.

- Learn to be more flexible. Being too rigid with a distractible student will only create conflict, anxiety, and tension.

- Call on the student more often than on others without making it too obvious. Keeping the student on her toes will increase the chances that her attention will stay focused.

- Offer the student extra help before or after school to deal with her distractibility.

- If necessary, consult with the school counseling or social work staff or the school psychologist about the possibility of setting up a behavior modification program or contract.

- If the problem is severe and persists, consult the school's pupil personnel team.

Drop-Out Potential

Why Students
May Exhibit This Behavior

ACADEMIC   Students who fail academically may feel there is no reason to stay in school. For adolescents who cannot succeed, there is a real feeling of helplessness. After repeated failures, they decide that dropping out is their only option.

ENVIRONMENTAL   Adolescents who have serious problems at home may feel the need to drop out. Reasons for this include feeling that they can never succeed in their parents' eyes and being unable to live up to the standards set by brothers and sisters.

INTELLECTUAL   Students who have low or below-average IQs may be unable to succeed at school. Their repeated attempts lead to failure and frustration. In the process, they become convinced that school is no longer worth the effort.

LINGUISTIC   Students who struggle with language may not understand or be able to complete school assignments. After a while, the frustration and anxiety become unbearable. Such students decide it is better to drop out than to endure more failures.

MEDICAL   Students with medical problems may have greater difficulty in school than their peers who do not have these problems. Also, excessive absences can contribute to these students' falling behind in their studies. In brief, these students have a high potential for dropping out because they have expended so much energy on their medical problems that they do not have the energy to continue with school.

PERCEPTUAL   See *Linguistic.*

PSYCHOLOGICAL   Adolescents who feel as though life is unfair, have suicidal tendencies, are seriously depressed, or have other such problems cannot focus on schoolwork, nor do they often care. Slowly, their academic performance deteriorates. Dropping out is an escape from a real and very difficult world.

SOCIAL   When adolescents feel they are not accepted by their peers, they may decide school is not for them. Social inadequacies make their lives at school painful and nonproductive. As a result, they may decide to drop out.

What to Do

Dropping out of school is a very serious problem. If as a teacher you suspect that a student may drop out, it is imperative that you contact the school psychologist and/or principal right away. Most schools have interventions for at-risk students. Parent involvement will also be important.

Excuses

Why Students
<u>*May Exhibit This Behavior*</u>

ACADEMIC   Excuses for not doing homework, not finishing class work, forgetting books, and so on are very common with students who have serious learning problems, especially if these avoidance behaviors constitute a pattern. Other avoidance behaviors may include selective forgetting (usually centering around areas of learning that may be creating frustration), habitually forgetting to write down assignments, taking hours to complete homework, having trouble getting started with tasks, frequently bringing home unfinished class work, consistently leaving long-term assignments until the last minute, and frequently complaining of headaches or stomachaches before school. You can determine the seriousness of the problem by considering the frequency, duration, and intensity of the symptoms.

ENVIRONMENTAL   Some adolescents employ excuses to avoid negative parental reactions, especially in homes where excessive corporal punishment may be used. Other students resort to excuses to avoid losing status within their families or disappointing their parents.

INTELLECTUAL   Excuses may be a means of coping and surviving for students with limited ability who want to avoid negative peer reactions and embarrassment.

LINGUISTIC   See *Perceptual.*

PERCEPTUAL   Students with perceptual deficits may not be able to process information as quickly as others and may resort to excuses to cover up their inadequacies.

PSYCHOLOGICAL   Students commonly make excuses when their energies are drained by serious problems, conflicts, fears, and so on. They have very little energy available, and what remains is used for creative avoidance. "Illogical logic" in a student's excuses—the excuse is blatantly illogical, but to the student it is very logical—is cause for concern. Such self-deception is very common in anxiety-driven students. In some students, habitual use of excuses is nothing more than lying. This pattern may reflect a pathology that is deeply ingrained and may indicate a more serious problem that needs to be discussed with the school psychologist.

SOCIAL   Students who fear social ridicule, rejection, or loss of status may resort to excuses, which, in their minds, preserve their social positions.

What to Do

- All students make excuses. As long as it does not happen frequently, it is something that should be expected. However, excuses can be problematic if they result in lying. Therefore, we will treat habitual excuses as an avoidance pattern that may include lying. We recommend taking the following steps:

  1. It is important to obtain complete information about the situation at hand. You do not want to draw conclusions or make accusations without being at least reasonably sure that what the student has offered constitutes an unfounded excuse.

  2. If you believe that a student has lied, speak to him privately to avoid embarrassing him. If you address the matter in front of anyone—student or adult—you increase the chances of the student's continuing to lie because he will not want to be publicly humiliated.

  3. If you are reasonably sure that lying has taken place, do not use entrapment. In other words, do not try to trick the student into admitting that his excuses are really lies.

  4. Be diplomatic, clear, and direct in confronting the student with what you know to be the facts. Stay calm, but be firm to show the student that you are serious.

  5. After explaining your point of view, ask the student if he wants to rethink what was said. Don't put him on the spot if there is no immediate response. Say, "We will talk

about this again some time today when you are ready, but we will definitely talk about it today."

6. If the student admits to having made a false excuse, say that you appreciate her honesty, then tell her what the consequences will be. The consequences should be appropriate and predetermined.

7. If the student does not admit to lying, you must act on the overwhelming evidence. Tell the student that the evidence indicates that lying did take place and that class rules have been violated, then administer the consequences.

- If the problem is severe or persists, consult the school counseling or social work staff, the school psychologist, or the pupil personnel team.

Fatigue

Why Students
May Exhibit This Behavior

ACADEMIC For most students, schoolwork requires great mental energy. Even those who do well must exert some mental energy to maintain their standards. However, students for whom school does not come easily need twice as much energy to complete assignments. Eventually, their energy is drained, and they suffer from general fatigue.

ENVIRONMENTAL Many adolescents do not get enough sleep at home, whether because bedtimes are not enforced or because the students are emotionally drained by family conflicts or difficulties.

INTELLECTUAL Students with limited intelligence will require extra energy to complete assignments successfully. Eventually, the effort takes its toll, and they begin to tire out. For gifted students, on the other hand, fatigue may actually result from the boredom that comes from not being challenged.

LINGUISTIC Students who do not understand the language of instruction well can rapidly become bored because they simply do not know what is going on in the classroom. Their boredom leads to fatigue.

MEDICAL Some medical conditions can create fatigue, as can medications that students may be taking.

PERCEPTUAL See *Linguistic.*

PSYCHOLOGICAL Students suffering from depression, low self-esteem, or anxiety may experience fatigue: Such a state becomes emotionally draining for anyone. Also, students suffering from psychological problems may be on medications that may create drowsiness.

SOCIAL Some students try to be everywhere doing countless things simultaneously. Their excessive social involvement can create a general state of fatigue and exhaustion.

What to Do

- Ask the school nurse if a medical condition might be causing the student's fatigue.

- Ask the school psychologist about possible circumstances underlying the pattern of fatigue. If the fatigue is the result of avoidance, withdrawal, or some other psychological problem, then building confidence is crucial. The student who uses fatigue as an avoidance mechanism needs a foundation of successful experiences accrued over time, as well as the appropriate social tools, to be an active participant in the classroom.

- Speak with the student privately in a comfortable setting. Explain that you are aware of his difficulty and that you want to help.

- Have the student work in groups so that the group energy will create excitement for him. Have the groups work on simple goal-oriented tasks that will ensure success and give the student the feeling of belonging and group accomplishment.

- Provide different small-group activities so that the student has the opportunity to work with all the members of her class. Assign groups and monitor the interactions to ensure protection and success.

- Consult with the school counseling or social work staff or the school psychologist about including the student in a social skills group to increase his activity level.

- If the problem is severe and persists, consult with the school's pupil personnel team.

Fear of Adults

Why Students
May Exhibit This Behavior

ACADEMIC   Some students generally fear authority figures, including teachers. A student may have had one teacher who was extremely hard on her and may have generalized from this teacher to all teachers.

ENVIRONMENTAL   Adolescents whose parents are overly strict or who are neglected or abused may have learned to fear all authority figures.

INTELLECTUAL   Some students with limited intellectual abilities cannot meet the expectations that parents or teachers have established for them. Their sense of failure gives rise to fear.

LINGUISTIC   Students with language difficulties may fear that teachers will ridicule them or be overly critical of their speech or writing.

MEDICAL   Adolescents with medical problems may fear adults because they believe that adults are to blame for their problems. The doctor who cannot cure the adolescent may be looked upon as the enemy, as the adolescent becomes increasingly afraid of anticipated pain. Also, a medically frail student may have in her life an adult who does not know how to handle the situation and behaves in a way that creates fear.

PERCEPTUAL   See *Linguistic.*

PSYCHOLOGICAL   Some students may fear adults for various psychological reasons, and low self-esteem can aggravate the fear. Adults can create great psychological damage in students—for instance, by giving the message that they are worthless. Other students with depression or anxiety disorders may fear the authority figures in their lives because they believe that no one understands them.

SOCIAL   Some students may have parents who expect them to be involved in numerous social activities, but they may be afraid of or indifferent to the activities. These feelings can become manifested in a fear of adults.

What to Do

- Understand that the student's fear of authority is involuntary. It will take time and patience for her to understand that you are a person to be trusted.

- Ask the school psychologist about any extenuating circumstances underlying the student's fear of adults.

- Help the student feel comfortable in the classroom by building her confidence. The fearful student needs a foundation of successful experiences accrued over time, as well as the appropriate social tools, to be an active participant in the classroom.

- Speak with the student privately in a comfortable setting. Explain that you are aware of her difficulty and that you want to help. Try to assure her that all adults need not be feared. Encourage her to verbalize why she fears certain adults in her life.

- If the problem is severe and persists, consult with the school's pupil personnel team.

Fear of New Situations

Why Students
May Exhibit This Behavior

ACADEMIC Some students experience failure in multiple academic areas in spite of their best efforts. Eventually, they become afraid to take chances in new situations because doing so normally just brings on negative results.

ENVIRONMENTAL Some adolescents live in homes where everything is done for them, they are afraid of their parents, or they do not feel protected by the significant adults in their lives. In any of these cases, an adolescent lacks the confidence and the self-esteem to take chances. The fear of what may happen supersedes the sense of good that might come from taking a risk.

INTELLECTUAL Students with limited intellectual abilities may be afraid of new situations because they have difficulties adapting. They lack the mechanisms for coping with change and are thus more comfortable with habit.

LINGUISTIC Students with language difficulties may fear situations involving their speaking abilities because they anticipate embarrassment or ridicule. They may generalize and begin to fear any and all new situations, especially those involving language skills.

MEDICAL Students with medical problems may fear new situations when they believe risk taking may harm them physically. For example, a student with severe asthma may always be afraid of outdoor activities because he once had a very bad asthma attack, or a diabetic student may be afraid to go on a school trip because she is worried about her blood sugar level.

PERCEPTUAL Students with perceptual difficulties may fear situations involving their abilities to read, write, speak, or discriminate between left and right. They anticipate embarrassment or ridicule. In the process, they begin to generalize their fears to any and all new situations.

106

PSYCHOLOGICAL Students with low self-esteem normally question their abilities and experience anxiety when called on to do new things.

SOCIAL Some students want so desperately to fit in that they will participate only in activities in which they know they will succeed. They are hesitant to take risks for fear of being ridiculed by peers if they fail.

What to Do

- Remember that the student's behavior fulfills a protective function. Therefore, attempting to force him into new situations will only create conflict, anxiety, and tension.
- Ask the school psychologist about possible circumstances underlying the student's fearfulness.
- Remember that in order for a fearful student to open up, he must feel comfortable and confident in the classroom. The fearful student needs a foundation of successful experiences accrued over time, as well as appropriate social tools to be an active participant in the classroom.
- Speak with the student privately in a comfortable setting. Explain that you are aware of his difficulty and that you want to help.
- Help the student build confidence through practical guidance. For instance, involve him in small groups and then gradually increase the group size. Initially, group him with students who tend to be sensitive to others' feelings. Have those groups work on simple goal-oriented tasks that will give the student the feeling of belonging and group accomplishment. Assign the groups and monitor the interactions to ensure protection and success.
- Offer different types of small-group activities so that the student has the opportunity to work with all the members of his class.
- Speak with the school counseling or social work staff or the school psychologist about including the student in a social skills group.
- If the problem is severe and persists, consult with the school's pupil personnel team.

Fighting

Why Students
May Exhibit This Behavior

ACADEMIC   Unrelieved frustration usually leads to anger; students who suffer from academic frustration may displace their anger toward others because they cannot succeed academically as they know others can.

ENVIRONMENTAL   In some students, aggression may stem from stressors experienced at home. These may include unrealistic expectations from parents, inappropriate parenting, inability to emulate a sibling's success, or—in the most serious of cases—physical or emotional abuse.

INTELLECTUAL   Students with limited intelligence may resort to aggressive behavior in attempts to offset feelings of inadequacy and gain status.

LINGUISTIC   Students who have difficulty communicating in language may release their frustration through behavior instead of through words.

MEDICAL   In some students, aggression may be due to neurological conditions, chemical imbalances, or problems with medication.

PERCEPTUAL   Students who have difficulty perceiving the world as others do may be highly frustrated. They may misperceive others' words and actions and respond with physically aggressive behavior.

PSYCHOLOGICAL   Certain psychological states (low self-esteem, anxiety, depressed mood, etc.) can create feelings of inadequacy and increased tension in some students. They may act out their inner stress through aggressive behavior. Also, certain types of behavior disorders (conduct disorder, oppositional defiant disorder, impulse disorder, etc.) can lead to such behavior.

SOCIAL Some students may feel rejected and inadequate—as if they do not fit in. They may act out these feelings through physical aggression toward others. Other students may believe that aggressive "tough guy" behavior will gain them social status.

What to Do

- When physical aggression leads to a fight in or outside the classroom, it is crucial to remain calm. Doing so will set the tone of control and establish you as the leader of the class.
- Isolate the fighting students for safety purposes.
- Place the students in a setting that allows for some form of supervision. For example, send them separately to the principal's office or the office of the school psychologist, counselor, or social worker.
- Allow the students uninterrupted quiet time to calm down. This will prevent the possibility of further escalation and give them a chance to collect themselves and save face.
- Help the physically aggressive student label the likely trigger for her behavior. Encouraging her to express her thoughts and feelings verbally reduces the need for physical venting of frustration.
- Suggest alternate means of resolving future conflicts. Many students who consistently fight know no other way to handle difficult and stressful situations.
- If aggression is a consistent pattern, confer with the student's parents.
- Consult with the school counseling or social work staff or the school psychologist. Explore the possibility of developing a behavioral contract or setting up a behavior modification program for the student.
- If the problem is severe and persists, consult with the school's pupil personnel team.

Follower Role

Why Students
May Exhibit This Behavior

ACADEMIC   Students may be reluctant to take their turns exercising leadership in group academic projects because of fear that their ideas will not be accepted.

ENVIRONMENTAL   With respect to leadership, students may emulate the behavior they see at home. Some students view the authority figures in their lives as independent thinkers. Others see their parents and relatives as followers and tend to be followers themselves.

INTELLECTUAL   Most leaders are smart. For students with limited intellectual ability, it is much easier to follow the group than to try to impose their own beliefs. Also, students with below-average intellect may lack the creativity and quickness associated with leadership.

LINGUISTIC   To be a leader, one must communicate one's ideas. Students with language difficulties may feel very uncomfortable speaking their minds or countering others' views.

PSYCHOLOGICAL   Many students lack the internal strength and confidence to be leaders. They are insecure about voicing their opinions because they primarily want to be accepted. The prospect of creating controversy and trying to lead others in new directions can be threatening, and they content themselves with following.

SOCIAL   Most adolescents just want to fit in socially with their peers. They don't want to stand out in any way. They feel more secure following others' leadership than stepping up and speaking their minds.

What to Do

- When a student is reluctant to take his turn as leader, speak with him privately. Discuss how he is doing and how he feels about himself.

- Give the student leadership tasks at which you know he can excel. This will enhance his self-confidence and his willingness to lead in the future.

- Give the student all forms of positive reinforcement. You may want to ask your colleagues for suggestions.

- Confer with the parents to see if anything has happened to undercut the youngster's self-confidence.

- If necessary, consult with the school counseling or social work staff or the school psychologist about the possibility of including the student in a self-esteem group or setting up a behavior modification program for him.

- If the problem is severe and persists, consult with the school's pupil personnel team.

Forgetfulness

Why Students
May Exhibit This Behavior

ACADEMIC   Some students who experience academic failure hate school so much that they "forget" what is required of them in terms of class work or homework.

ENVIRONMENTAL   Students from families with significant problems have many worries and concerns. Remembering homework assignments and due dates is not a high priority in the context of other issues.

INTELLECTUAL   Students with limited intelligence may have memory problems, which can obviously lead them to forget information, assignments, due dates, and so on.

LINGUISTIC   Students with language difficulties may appear forgetful, whereas in reality they may simply not have understood their assignments. To avoid admitting that they do not understand what is going on in the classroom, they state that they forgot to do what was required.

MEDICAL   Students with attention deficit/hyperactivity disorder (AD/HD) may have great difficulty remembering things. Also, forgetfulness can be a side effect of certain medications.

PERCEPTUAL   See *Linguistic*.

PSYCHOLOGICAL   Low self-esteem, denial, depression, anxiety, and fear can all lead to forgetfulness. More often than not, if a medical problem is not to blame, students forget because they are preoccupied with issues in their lives. Anxiety and depression are psychologically draining and thus interfere with the assimilation and retention of information.

SOCIAL   Some students become forgetful regarding schoolwork because they are preoccupied with their extracurricular activities and social calendars.

What to Do

- Confer with the school nurse and the student's parents to find out whether some medical problem may be causing the difficulty with memory.

- Limit the amount of auditory and visual stimuli in the classroom so that the student does not have too many things to memorize and retain.

- Give verbal praise when the student remembers something important.

- Try to get involved with the student's activities when she needs to stay on task. Your interaction may increase her chances of remembering information and procedures.

- Have the student work in groups with others who do not have problems with forgetfulness.

- Have the student write down exactly what she must do. Often, students become forgetful because they are distracted by other stimuli. Having written directions enables the student to get back on track and complete her task.

- Seat the student in the front of the room to minimize her chances of being distracted by other stimuli.

- Offer the student extra help before or after school to deal with her memory problem.

- If necessary, consult with the school's counseling or social work staff, the school psychologist, or the pupil personnel team.

Lack of Friends

Why Students
May Exhibit This Behavior

ACADEMIC   Students may lack friends because of extremely high or low academic ability. Some students are so intelligent that peers cannot relate to them. Students who perform poorly in school may be unable to make friends either because they are devoting all of their energy to keeping up in the classroom or because they are shunned by peers. In another type of classroom dynamic, students may turn away from others who are visibly different. For example, a student who is blind or uses a wheelchair may have few friends not because of personality but, sadly, because peers may avoid making friends with him out of ignorance about disabilities.

ENVIRONMENTAL   Some adolescents may lack friends because their environments are not conducive to friendship. For example, an adolescent whose parents forbid him to go outside after school may not have the chance to form strong bonds with other neighborhood kids. An adolescent who lives in a neighborhood with no one in his age group may lack friends for this reason.

INTELLECTUAL   Students with intellectual limitations may be in special classes and even in separate classrooms. They have trouble making friends because they are not doing the class work that most of their peers are doing, and they do not understand what the others are doing in any event.

LINGUISTIC   If students cannot communicate their ideas and feelings to others, they may feel too insecure to try to make friends. Also, students with obvious language problems, such as stuttering, may avoid reaching out to others because they fear embarrassment and ridicule.

MEDICAL   Students whose medical problems cause them to be absent from school for long periods miss many events and opportunities to make friends. They simply are not around their peers long enough to form strong bonds.

PERCEPTUAL   Things that come easily for most students require much more work for those with perceptual difficulties. Because they cannot keep pace, other students may not want to be friends with them.

PSYCHOLOGICAL   Many students lack friends because they lack confidence and self-esteem. Their poor opinions of themselves cause them to retreat. Other students lack friends because they have deep-rooted psychological problems and behave in ways that peers find unacceptable.

SOCIAL   Some adolescents lack the skills needed to interact with groups successfully. They may do fine in one-on-one relation-ships, but in social situations they fail. Adolescents who have this problem tend to be shunned by most of their classmates.

What to Do

- Try to identify a classmate who might be able to become friends with the student. Seat this student next to the friend-less student. This may spark a friendship or put him at ease.

- If the foregoing strategy does not work, speak privately with the student about his difficulty in making friends. You could ask the student to write a paragraph describing himself so that you may better understand his thoughts and feelings.

- Try to involve the student in more group activities. In a small group, he may improve his ability to relate to others.

- Rotate groups every few weeks so that the student gets the chance to meet all of his classmates in a comfortable setting.

- If necessary, confer with the parents. Perhaps there are exter-nal circumstances underlying the student's difficulties.

- Consult with the school counseling or social work staff or the school psychologist. This student may need group or individual therapy, both in and out of school.

- If the problem is severe and persists, consult with the school's pupil personnel team.

Gang Participation

Why Students
May Exhibit This Behavior

ACADEMIC Constant academic failure may lower an adolescent's self-worth to the extent that gang participation, with its anti-authority and anti-school messages, may alleviate feelings of inadequacy. Feelings of inadequacy and insecurity are directed into anger toward a system that "makes" the adolescent feel bad about himself.

ENVIRONMENTAL Adolescents may join gangs if they come from homes that do not provide guidance or boundaries. Gangs offer such adolescents rules, connections, and boundaries, even though such affiliations are antisocial. The gang family usually provide what the adolescent's family of origin cannot.

PSYCHOLOGICAL Students participate in gang activity for several psychological reasons: to feel connection, to achieve a sense of empowerment, and to express anger felt toward people in authority. Gang participation also may serve as a rejection of values held by the family.

SOCIAL The need in adolescence for affiliation is so strong that "any port in a storm" may do, regardless of antisocial atmosphere.

What to Do

Never attempt to handle any issue dealing with gangs or gang participation on your own. This is a serious and potentially dangerous situation. We highly recommend that gang concerns be handled through an administrative process. If gang behavior is overt or exhibited in your classroom, speak with the principal or the dean of students. If you suspect an individual student of gang involvement, avoid confronting that student. Rather, speak with the school psychologist to determine whether academic or personal problems are a factor, then make appropriate referrals.

Hesitance

Why Students
May Exhibit This Behavior

ACADEMIC   Limited ability and poor academic performance can engender feelings of inadequacy. Lack of success and self-confidence can make a student hesitant to try anything new.

ENVIRONMENTAL   Students whose parents are overly critical or verbally abusive may be hesitant in order to avoid saying or doing something that they know will stir up problems.

INTELLECTUAL   Intellectual limitations can reduce a student's self-confidence and make him hesitant, especially if his efforts have consistently elicited negative responses.

LINGUISTIC   Certain language disorders or articulation problems may make a student hesitant to communicate for fear of negative reactions.

MEDICAL   In some cases, an organic disorder can affect a student's ability or willingness to interact with peers. Also, some students with serious medical conditions may hesitate to get involved with others because their conditions prevent them from succeeding as others do.

PERCEPTUAL   Students with certain types of processing problems have trouble keeping up with others. They become hesitant because they are afraid that their efforts will end in failure or elicit ridicule.

PSYCHOLOGICAL   Severe anxiety and tension can result in hesitant behavior by way of self-absorption. In such cases, what appears to be hesitancy is rather indifference to the activities and concerns of others. Also, low self-esteem can create hesitant behavior. Students with low self-esteem may not take chances because they do not believe that they can succeed.

SOCIAL   Students may be hesitant if they fear rejection by peers, lack confidence in social situations, have poor social skills, fear being victimized, or do not understand social rules and norms.

What to Do

- Remember that hesitancy fulfills some protective function. Therefore, attempting to force a student into a particular situation will only create tremendous conflict, anxiety, and tension.

- Meet with the school psychologist to determine whether there are any special circumstances underlying the student's hesitancy (e.g., home issues, trauma, previous academic failure).

- Help the hesitant student open up gradually by making him feel comfortable in the classroom. At times, this may be like coaxing a frightened turtle out of its shell. It requires patience.

- Help the student build confidence over time. The hesitant student needs a foundation of successful experiences as well as the appropriate social tools to be an active participant in the classroom.

- Meet with the student privately in a comfortable setting. Explain that you are aware of his difficulty in both academic and social situations and that you want to help.

- Provide practical guidance. For instance, involve the hesitant student in small groups and then gradually increase the group size. Initially, group him with students who you know are sensitive to others' feelings.

- Have the groups work on simple goal-oriented tasks that will give the student the feeling of belonging and group accomplishment. Assign the groups and monitor progress to ensure protection and success.

- Provide a variety of small-group activities so that the student has the opportunity to work with all the members of his class.

- Consult with the school counseling or social work staff or the school psychologist about including the student in a social skills group.

- If the problem is severe and persists, confer with the school's pupil personnel team.

Failure to Complete Homework

Why Students
May Exhibit This Behavior

ACADEMIC   The multiple reasons students may not do homework can be summed up under two possibilities: First, the homework is too difficult, and students give up. Second, they do not feel like doing homework because they find it boring.

ENVIRONMENTAL   Many environmental factors can interfere with students' completing their homework. They may lack parental supervision, they may be distracted by family problems, the family may not place a high priority on education, or the home environment may not be conducive to studying.

INTELLECTUAL   Students with limited intellectual ability may become frustrated because they work more slowly than their peers. They may eventually decide to give up altogether. Gifted students, on the other hand, may stop doing homework because they see no point in studying material that they have already mastered.

LINGUISTIC   Students who have difficulty either understanding language or expressing themselves verbally may become overwhelmed. They may avoid doing homework altogether because they feel destined to fail regardless of their efforts.

MEDICAL   Some adolescents may not be doing homework because of medical problems such as visual or hearing impairments, brain damage, or nervous system injury, to name just a few.

PERCEPTUAL   Some students with perceptual problems have great difficulty decoding and encoding words (the classic example being the dyslexic student). What would take most students an hour takes these students 5 to 6 hours, and they still do not finish their assignments. Intolerable frustration may lead them eventually to give up.

PSYCHOLOGICAL   There are many possible psychological reasons students do not complete their homework. First, they may be unable to handle the responsibility and demands of homework and consequently become highly frustrated. Second, they may be engaging in a form of passive-aggressive behavior to upset their parents. Finally, they may be trying to gain negative attention for not doing certain things that they know are important to the authority figures in their lives.

SOCIAL   Some students neglect their homework because they are overly involved with their friends and activities. For them, social life has a higher priority than academics. Other students may be responding to negative peer pressure: Their social group thinks homework is "not cool," and they don't want to be different.

What to Do

- Confer with the parents to determine what factors may be contributing to the student's homework problem. Keep in mind that the parents may have tried everything and may themselves be totally frustrated. Try to be solution oriented and work as a team.

- Ask the parents to establish a scheduled homework time so that homework becomes a part of the student's normal routine.

- Speak privately with the student. Ask her what she thinks is behind her failure to complete homework. Assure the student that you are acting out of concern and that you are there to help.

- Review the student's homework assignments to determine if they are too difficult or if the time allowed to complete them is not sufficient.

- Try giving shorter assignments that may increase the student's gratification and feelings of success. In rebuilding confidence, you may have to go backward before going forward.

- Keep in mind that all homework should reinforce what is learned in the classroom. Some students may not be able to do assigned homework because they did not understand the information or concepts in the first place.

- Assure the student that doing something is better than doing nothing. Also, tell her that if she is unsure about an assignment, she can bring a note from a parent explaining the circumstances.
- Allow the student to use alternative forms of output—tape recordings, posters, and the like—to demonstrate knowledge and understanding.

Taking Too Long to Complete Homework

Why Students
May Exhibit This Behavior

ACADEMIC   Some students have great difficulties in certain academic subjects. When they have homework in these subjects, it can take them much more time than would normally be expected because they have so much trouble grasping the concepts.

ENVIRONMENTAL   Some students take an inordinately long time to do their homework because their parents do not set time limits for its completion.

INTELLECTUAL   Students with limited intellectual abilities need extra time to interpret directions, ingest information, and respond with the required output.

LINGUISTIC   When students do not comprehend the language of instruction adequately, they will invariably take much longer than others to do their work.

MEDICAL   Students with certain medical conditions may not be able to do their homework in a sustained manner. This difficulty may be due to attention deficit/hyperactivity disorder (AD/HD) or some other medical condition that makes it impossible to sit and concentrate for long periods.

PERCEPTUAL   Students with perceptual difficulties may have to spend extra time interpreting homework assignments and determining how to do the work properly.

PSYCHOLOGICAL   Students with psychological problems such as depression, anxiety, or low self-esteem are easily engrossed in thoughts of their problems when they sit down to do homework. The competing thoughts prevent them from completing their assignments in normal periods of time.

SOCIAL   Some students have so many social activities going on after school that they cannot stay seated long enough to finish their work. Consequently, they do homework in bits and pieces over many hours.

What to Do

- In all likelihood, the problem with homework has been reported to you by the parent. You may want to offer the parent the following suggestions:

   1. Establish a homework schedule. For some adolescents, the responsibility for deciding when to do homework may be too great. Help your adolescent decide the best time to do homework, and help him adhere to the schedule.

   2. Prioritize assignments. Deciding what to do first can be a major chore. Help your adolescent by determining the order in which assignments are to be completed.

   3. Do not sit next to your adolescent while he does homework. Because the same "assistance" is not available in the classroom, you can best help by acting as a resource person to whom the adolescent may turn when necessary. When the problem is solved or the question answered, the youngster should resume working independently.

   4. Acknowledge correct responses first. When your adolescent brings you a paper to check, state how well he did on the correct problems, spelling words, and so on. When you see incorrect responses, say something like "I'll bet if you go back and check these over, you may get a different answer."

   5. Never let homework drag on all night. The only thing gained if adolescents are allowed to linger on homework hour after hour with very little performance is a strong feeling of inadequacy. If your youngster is unable to progress on a given evening, end the work period after a reasonable time and write the teacher a note explaining the circumstances.

Note: These homework suggestions are from R. Pierangelo, *The Special Educator's Book of Lists,* 1995, Upper Saddle River, NJ: Prentice Hall. Adapted by permission.

6. Discuss homework questions before your adolescent reads an assigned portion of text. This will help him look for important information while reading.

7. Check small portions of the assignment. Have your adolescent do, for example, five problems and then check them with you. The youngster may benefit from the immediate gratification. Moreover, if he is doing the assignment incorrectly, the error can be detected and explained early in the process.

8. Record assigned reading on tape. Research indicates that the more senses involved in the input, the greater the chance students will retain information. You might, for example, tape science or social studies chapters so that your youngster can listen while reading in the textbook.

9. Be cautious about negative nonverbal messages. People communicate many messages, especially negative ones, involuntarily and without realizing it. A sensitive adolescent will pick up a negative message from a raised eyebrow or a parent's perceived inattentiveness during the homework time.

10. Avoid finishing assignments for your adolescent. Adolescents tend to feel inadequate when parents finish their homework. If your youngster cannot complete an assignment and has honestly tried, write the teacher a note explaining the circumstances.

11. Be alert to possible signs of more serious learning problems. Certain symptoms indicating the possibility of more serious learning problems may show up during homework time. They include constant avoidance of homework, forgetting to bring home assignments, taking hours to do homework, procrastination, low tolerance for frustration, labored writing, poor spelling, and the like. If you notice a pattern of such symptoms, talk to the classroom teacher, the school psychologist, or the resource room teacher.

12. Check homework at the end of the study time. This will ease your adolescent's concerns about bringing incorrect homework to school. It also provides a feeling of accomplishment, a source of positive attention, and a sense of security.

Impulsivity

Why Students
May Exhibit This Behavior

ACADEMIC Some students become very excited when they know the answers to questions. They have great difficulty raising their hands and waiting to be called on. If they are not taught acceptable classroom behavior, the impulsivity becomes persistent and self-reinforcing.

ENVIRONMENTAL Adolescents who are desperate for attention may try to grab it the moment it becomes available. Their impulsive behavior assures them that they will be noticed by parents, siblings, or others. This pattern of behavior can spill over into the school environment.

INTELLECTUAL See *Psychological.*

MEDICAL Perhaps the most common condition associated with impulsivity is attention deficit/hyperactivity disorder (AD/HD). Students with AD/HD tend to be distractible and to have great difficulty focusing on tasks at hand or following through on directions. They also tend to act without thinking.

PSYCHOLOGICAL Students who are impulsive may be incapable of restraining themselves from acting before thinking. Such students act on their feelings rather than projecting the consequences of their behaviors.

SOCIAL In social situations, students may want to do the first thing that others do. They may follow the group without any concern for consequences. Their impulsivity here is due to their desire to be accepted and to fit in with their peers.

What to Do

- Ask the school psychologist whether the student has been diagnosed with AD/HD or has ever received special education services.

- Ask the school nurse whether the student is on any medication to counteract impulsivity (e.g., Ritalin).

- If neither of the foregoing is the case, speak privately with the student and ask her why she acts so impulsively. Many students do so because they are seeking attention. Explain to the student that you recognize what she is doing. Establish some way to signal to her when you are ready to call on her.

- Explain to the student the class rules and appropriate classroom behavior. It is possible that the student has not experienced the type of structure necessary to function at this grade level.

- Because impulsive behavior often is manifested consistently, it is important to expect such behavior from the student. You should plan what to do if her impulsivity affects the class and administer the appropriate consequences if need be.

- If the situation is seriously affecting the student's social, emotional, or academic functioning, contact the parents. However, do not discuss the idea of medication with the parents. Even if you think medication is appropriate, this is not your role nor your area of expertise.

- If necessary, consult with the school's counseling or social work staff, the school psychologist, or the pupil personnel team.

Inconsistency

Why Students
May Exhibit This Behavior

ACADEMIC   Some students naturally do better in certain subjects than in others. However, in students with learning disabilities, the contrast between academic strengths and weaknesses may be pronounced.

ENVIRONMENTAL   Some students are inconsistent because they experience inconsistency at home: Their parents vacillate between strictness and indifference. Also, students of divorced parents who are involved in shared custodial arrangements may be inconsistent because their environments change at intervals.

INTELLECTUAL   Students may have strengths and weaknesses in different intellectual processes; inconsistent performance may reflect these variations.

MEDICAL   Medical problems can cause emotional ups and downs—and inconsistent performance. Moreover, students with medical problems may have frequent absences that keep them from doing well on a consistent basis.

PERCEPTUAL   Perceptual difficulties may affect a student in certain areas but not others. When the student is able to grasp things the way others do, his performance is strong; in other areas, he falters.

PSYCHOLOGICAL   In some students, emotional disorders cause mood swings that lead to frequent fluctuations in behavior. In other students, inconsistent behavior is due to parental alcoholism or drug use. If a parent is sober, the student may excel in school the next day. But if the parent is high and possibly aggressive, the student's next day may be horrible.

SOCIAL   Varied social contacts can lead to inconsistent behavior. For example, if on Tuesdays a student hangs out with peers who take school seriously, he may get his homework done. But if on

Wednesdays he hangs out with a "bad bunch," homework may be neglected because it is not valued by that group.

What to Do

- Try to discern patterns or themes in the student's inconsistency.

- Speak privately with the student about the areas of inconsistency you observe. (Be advised that this may be more difficult with younger adolescents.)

- If the student has a learning disability, keep in mind that behavior may vary with the academic subject matter. For example, a student with a reading disability may become agitated, act out, or withdraw right before class reading time. However, the same student may be outgoing and responsible during a subject in which he feels confident. If this is the pattern, then you may want to modify the manner of presentation, manner of response, level of difficulty, or frequency or length of assignments to ensure greater success and less avoidance.

- If there are times when any subject is avoided or incomplete on some days and on other days done according to class requirements, then the issue may have more to do with causes such as anxiety and tension. The pattern is like a lightbulb: sometimes on, sometimes off. If this is the case, then you may want to modify the frequency or length of assignments to ensure greater success and less avoidance.

- If you suspect that inconsistency may be a result of a learning disability, consult with the school counseling or social work staff, the school psychologist, or the pupil personnel team.

Inflexibility

ACADEMIC   Some students like to approach academic tasks in their own ways, and they can become very rigid. They like to stick with their proven methods, and they resist change.

ENVIRONMENTAL   A very strict and rigid home environment can create an adolescent who exhibits the same qualities because the adolescent copies what she sees. For example, if a parent is in the military, the home may be run like a tight ship or an army base.

INTELLECTUAL   A student with limited intelligence may have a narrow repertoire of approaches. Once the student has figured out a way to do something, she may be unwilling to change because she has experienced success. On the other hand, a gifted student may be very inflexible because she can solve problems in her head without writing them down as others do, even though the teacher wants to see all the intermediate steps on paper.

LINGUISTIC   When the language of instruction is not the student's first language, she may consider it unfair that she is obliged to learn another language in addition to keeping up with schoolwork. Feelings of resentment may lead to resistance and rigidity.

PSYCHOLOGICAL   Some students may be obsessive-compulsive or very fearful. These students may feel upset and insecure when challenged to take chances or risks. For them, inflexibility is actually a defense mechanism.

SOCIAL   Some students do not want to play by the rules; rather, they want to be the ones in charge. Their inflexibility is caused by a social need to be in control. Their behavior may eventually result in social problems and loss of friends.

What to Do

- Remember that a student exhibiting inflexibility feels very unsure of herself and her situation. Therefore, attempting to force her to engage will only create tremendous conflict, anxiety, and tension.

- Ask the school psychologist whether there are any particular circumstances underlying the student's inflexibility (e.g., home issues, trauma, previous academic failure).

- Speak privately with the student in a comfortable setting. Explain that you are aware of her difficulty and want to help.

- Help the student feel comfortable in the classroom by building her confidence. She needs a foundation of successful experiences accrued over time, as well as appropriate social tools, in order to be open to new ways of doing things.

- Have the student work in groups to help her build confidence. Have the groups work on simple goal-oriented tasks that will give the student the feeling of belonging and group accomplishment. Assign the groups and monitor progress to ensure protection and success.

- Provide the student with a variety of small-group activities so that she has the opportunity to work with all the members of her class.

- Consult with the school's counseling or social work staff or the school psychologist about the possibility of including the student in a social skills group or setting up a behavior modification program for her.

- If the problem is severe and persists, consult with the school's pupil personnel team.

Insecurity

Why Students
May Exhibit This Behavior

ACADEMIC   Students who do not experience academic success may feel very insecure. Their lack of confidence may eventually lead to learned helplessness: They give up on trying because they see all previous academic efforts as having led to failure.

ENVIRONMENTAL   Insecurity may be due to environmental deprivation resulting from loss of a parent, inadequate parenting, lack of nurturance, or parental reinforcement of immature behavior.

INTELLECTUAL   Students with limited intelligence may be insecure because they lack confidence in their abilities and consider themselves unlikely to succeed.

LINGUISTIC   Students with language difficulties may be very insecure when they are required to engage in some activity involving language. This fear can become generalized to great insecurity regarding their overall abilities.

MEDICAL   A student with a serious medical condition may be very insecure about his abilities if he has had limited opportunity to do things for himself.

PERCEPTUAL   Students with perceptual difficulties may be very insecure when they must engage in activities with others or in front of others. They fear that they will display weaknesses; this fear can be generalized to great insecurity regarding their overall abilities.

PSYCHOLOGICAL   Insecurity may stem from inadequate emotional development related to parental rejection, favoritism toward another sibling, tension between parents, and so on.

SOCIAL   Students may be insecure because they lack confidence in their abilities in social situations and activities. They may lack self-esteem and have great difficulty fitting in with their peers.

What to Do

- Remember that the insecure student is feeling very unsure of himself and his situation. Therefore, attempting to force him to engage will only create tremendous conflict, anxiety, and tension.

- Ask the school psychologist whether there are any particular circumstances underlying the student's insecurity (e.g., home issues, trauma, previous academic failure).

- Speak with the student privately in a comfortable setting. Explain that you are aware of his difficulty and want to help.

- Help the student feel comfortable in the classroom by gradually building his confidence. The insecure student needs a foundation of successful experiences accrued over time, as well as appropriate social tools, in order to be an active participant in the classroom.

- Have the student work in groups to help him build confidence. Have the groups work on simple goal-oriented tasks that will give the student the feeling of belonging and group accomplishment. Assign and monitor the groups to ensure protection and success.

- Provide a variety of small-group activities so that the student has the opportunity to work with all the members of his class.

- Consult with the school's counseling or social work staff or the school psychologist about the possibility of including the student in a social skills group or setting up a behavior modification program for him.

- If the problem is severe and persists, consult with the school's pupil personnel team.

Lack of Interest in School

ACADEMIC   Some students will do what is required of them whether they are interested or not. However, many students have great difficulty attending to academic tasks when they find the tasks boring.

ENVIRONMENTAL   Some adolescents will not be interested in school because of problems at home. These may range from simple household disorganization to a nasty divorce battle or even neglect or abuse. Home conflicts or problems exert a much more powerful pull than academic subjects, and adolescents subsequently lose interest in school in general.

INTELLECTUAL   In some students, lack of interest in school is due to limited intelligence. On the other hand, students with very high intelligence may have great difficulty maintaining interest in school because they rapidly become bored in a classroom designed for average students.

LINGUISTIC   Students who have difficulty understanding the language of instruction will likely have difficulty with their class work. They can rapidly become frustrated and give up, in the process losing interest in the subject matter.

MEDICAL   Students with serious medical problems may have no interest in academic work or school activities because they are totally focused on their medical conditions.

PERCEPTUAL   Students who do not see the world as others do can experience great frustration in trying to complete class work. The frustrations can eventually become overwhelming, leading them to lose interest in school.

PSYCHOLOGICAL   Students who suffer from depression or anxiety may lack the energy to focus on important school matters. They may simply not have the mental strength to become interested in anything.

SOCIAL   Some students are not interested in schoolwork because they are preoccupied with their social lives. They do not find academic work too difficult, but social concerns have higher priority for them.

What to Do

- Remember that a student who lacks interest in school is probably behaving in this manner for some protective reason. No student wishes to fail. A total lack of interest in school has roots that need to be explored.

- Ask the school psychologist whether there are any particular circumstances underlying the student's lack of interest (e.g., home issues, trauma, previous academic failure).

- Speak with the student privately in a comfortable setting. Explain that you are aware of her difficulty in academic and/or social situations and that you want to help.

- A student who lacks interest in school may really lack confidence. If this appears to be the case, help her build confidence gradually. This student needs a foundation of successful experiences, as well as appropriate social tools, in order to be an active participant in the classroom.

- Provide the student with a variety of small-group activities so that she has the opportunity to work with all the members of her class. Assign these groups and monitor the interactions to ensure protection and success.

- Consult with the school counseling or social work staff or the school psychologist about having the student join a social skills group.

- If the problem is severe and persists, consult the school's pupil personnel team.

Interrupting the Teacher

Why Students
May Exhibit This Behavior

ACADEMIC   There are students who do not understand many concepts and students who understand everything. In both groups are students who continually need to tell the teacher what they know or don't know.

ENVIRONMENTAL   Some adolescents get insufficient attention and recognition at home, and they seek attention from the teacher to compensate for this lack. Others get so much attention at home that they expect the same in the classroom. Either behavior leads to many interruptions for the teacher.

INTELLECTUAL   Students with limited intellectual abilities may constantly interrupt the teacher in their efforts to keep up in class.

LINGUISTIC   Students who frequently interrupt the teacher may do so because they do not understand the language the teacher is using. This could mean that the language is not their first language or that the teacher is speaking too quickly.

MEDICAL   Students with medical conditions may interrupt a teacher because they have physical needs that must be addressed. These could require minor measures, such as adjusting a seat or speaking more loudly, or more time-consuming ones, such as taking a student to the bathroom.

PERCEPTUAL   Students who cannot perceive things as others do, whether in visual or auditory terms, will often need extra help. If they have come to expect extra attention because of their perceptual problems, they may constantly interrupt the teacher.

PSYCHOLOGICAL   Some students have low self-esteem and need continual reassurance. Others have self-centered tendencies and an urge always to be in the spotlight. Still others may have needs that are not being met at home or with friends and may attempt to be close to the teacher in their efforts to get their needs met. Any of these situations can lead to constant interruptions.

SOCIAL   Some students need to be the center of attention. They may interrupt to show what they know or interrupt out of rebellion. In either case, they are likely seeking acceptance from their peers.

What to Do

- Speak privately with the student about what you are observing. Explain that his behavior in the classroom is becoming problematic and that it must stop.

- Give the student the opportunity to explain his side of the story. Does he interrupt constantly because he does not understand assignments or needs extra attention, or for some other reason?

- Try to get involved with the student as much as possible so that the potential for interruption is limited.

- Seat the student next to a classmate who can help him out and who is also compassionate and understanding.

- Let the student participate as much as possible in class discussions so that he feels that he is getting the attention he needs.

- If necessary, confer with the parents. Find out whether the problem behavior is school specific or occurs at home as well.

- When the student interrupts you, immediately let him know that the behavior is not acceptable.

- When the student refrains from interrupting you, praise him for appropriate behavior.

- If necessary, consult with the school counseling or social work staff or the school psychologist about the possibility of setting up a behavior modification program for the student.

- If the problem is severe and persists, consult with the school's pupil personnel team.

Intrusiveness

Why Students
May Exhibit This Behavior

ACADEMIC   When students are academically insecure or needy, when they feel as though they cannot do what is required of them, they may become intrusive both with the teacher and with their classmates.

ENVIRONMENTAL   Adolescents who come from large families or who for other reasons do not receive much attention may become intrusive in their efforts to feel secure.

INTELLECTUAL   Students with limited intelligence may be very insecure about their abilities and anxious about fitting in. They may become intrusive in efforts to keep pace with the class and be like their peers.

LINGUISTIC   Students with language problems may become intrusive to get the extra attention that they feel they need to succeed in the classroom or to find out what their classmates are doing.

MEDICAL   Students with medical conditions that inhibit them from doing things that others can do easily may intrude on others for assistance. Also, students with attention deficit/hyperactivity disorder (AD/HD) may exhibit very intrusive behavior because they tend to act on impulse.

PERCEPTUAL   See *Linguistic*.

PSYCHOLOGICAL   Students with low self-esteem may become intrusive as they seek reassurance, reinforcement, and extra attention.

SOCIAL   Some students try desperately to fit in with their peers but do not succeed, whether for psychological, physiological, academic, or other reasons. They resort to intrusive behavior in their efforts to gain access to social groups.

What to Do

- Speak privately with the student about what you are observing. Explain that her behavior is becoming problematic in the classroom and that it must stop.

- Give the student the opportunity to explain her side of the story. Find out why she is intruding on others. Is it because she does not understand assignments, needs extra attention, and so on?

- Get involved with the student as much as possible to take the focus off the other students.

- Seat the student next to a peer who can help her out and who is also compassionate and understanding.

- Let the student participate as much as possible in class discussions so that she feels that she is getting the attention she needs.

- If the intrusive behavior is consistently directed toward the same people, remove the student from their area. If necessary, seat her closer to you so that you can better supervise her.

- If necessary, confer with the parents. Find out if the intrusive behavior is school specific or occurs at home as well.

- When the student is intrusive, act immediately to let her know that the behavior is not acceptable.

- When the student refrains from intruding on others, praise her for appropriate behavior.

- If necessary, consult with the school's counseling or social work staff or the school psychologist about the possibility of setting up a behavior modification program for the student.

- If the problem is severe and persists, consult with the school's pupil personnel team.

Irresponsibility

Why Students
May Exhibit This Behavior

ACADEMIC Some students do not value academic work and are indifferent about the quality of their performance. Eventually, indifference leads to irresponsibility.

ENVIRONMENTAL In some homes, responsibility is not stressed and taught, and adolescents become spoiled. Because responsible behavior is not expected at home, they become irresponsible in all areas of life.

INTELLECTUAL Limited intelligence can interfere with a student's ability to understand that all behaviors have consequences. Failure to understand and anticipate consequences can lead to irresponsible behavior.

MEDICAL Certain neurological impairments may interfere with decision-making processes and thus lead to irresponsible behavior.

PSYCHOLOGICAL In some students, irresponsible behavior may manifest or mask other things that are bothering them. For instance, a student suffering from depression or anxiety may be too busy just trying to survive to be concerned about doing the responsible thing.

SOCIAL Adolescents who are very responsible individually can become irresponsible in groups. The classic example is the gang. More often than not, gang members are nice people in one-on-one interactions, yet collectively they can be mean-spirited and even violent.

What to Do

- Try to discern patterns or themes in the student's irresponsibility.

- Speak privately with the student about the areas in which
  you see him as being irresponsible. (This may be more difficult with younger adolescents.)

- If the student has a learning disability, be aware that irresponsibility may be associated with particular academic subjects. For example, a student with a reading disability may
  become agitated, act out, or withdraw just before class reading time. However, the same student may be outgoing during
  a subject in which he feels confident. If this is the pattern,
  then you may want to modify the manner of presentation,
  manner of response, level of difficulty, or frequency or length
  of assignments to ensure greater success and less avoidance.

- If there are times when any subject is avoided or incomplete
  on some days and on other days done according to class
  requirements, then the issue may have more to do with
  causes such as anxiety and tension. The pattern is like a
  lightbulb: sometimes on, sometimes off. If this is the case,
  then you may want to modify the frequency or length of
  assignments to ensure greater success and less avoidance.

- If you suspect that the student's irresponsibility may be due
  to a learning disability, consult with the school's counseling
  or social work staff, the school psychologist, or the pupil
  personnel team.

Poor Judgment

Why Students
May Exhibit This Behavior

ACADEMIC   Some students do not understand basic rules for school behavior, such as not looking at classmates' test papers and being quiet when the teacher is speaking. They may have poor judgment because they lack grounding in these rules.

ENVIRONMENTAL   Some adolescents have parents who exhibit extremely poor judgment, and they emulate the behavior they see modeled at home.

INTELLECTUAL   Limited intelligence can interfere with a student's ability to understand that all behaviors have consequences. Poor judgment can be the result.

LINGUISTIC   Students with language difficulties may exhibit poor judgment because they do not understand what is required of them and are unfamiliar with social rules and norms.

MEDICAL   Certain neurological impairments could interfere with decision-making processes and lead to poor judgment.

PERCEPTUAL   Students with perceptual difficulties may exhibit poor judgment because they see their own inappropriate behavior and decisions as acceptable.

PSYCHOLOGICAL   In some students, poor judgment may manifest or mask other things that are really bothering them. For instance, a student suffering from depression or anxiety may be too preoccupied with her own problems to be concerned about exercising good judgment.

SOCIAL   Some adolescents will go along with the group even if they know it is the wrong thing to do. For them, the need to be socially accepted outweighs the concern about doing what is wise.

What to Do

- If a student's poor judgment results in high-risk behavior, we strongly suggest that you immediately refer the student to the school psychologist, the principal, and/or the pupil personnel team.

- However, if the student's poor judgment does not involve high-risk behavior, please refer to the suggestions presented for irresponsibility, clowning, and bothering others. Poor judgment comes in many different symptomatic forms.

Laziness

Why Students
May Exhibit This Behavior

ACADEMIC   Students who appear lazy in school are often bored with the subject matter. Their boredom creates a sense of indifference, which manifests itself in laziness.

ENVIRONMENTAL   Some adolescents are lazy because their parents allow them to be. They are babied and catered to at home, and they expect similar treatment at school.

INTELLECTUAL   Gifted students may be lazy because they are not challenged in a classroom designed for average students. They do not feel the need to work hard because they know they can do well without putting in much effort.

LINGUISTIC   Language problems can create a sense of failure and frustration, and a student may respond by giving up. This reaction might be mistaken for laziness.

MEDICAL   A student with medical problems may have been nurtured to the point where he loses any form of independence. In the process, he may have learned laziness because he knows that effort will not be expected of him.

PERCEPTUAL   See *Linguistic.*

PSYCHOLOGICAL   Some students use laziness to aggravate parents and teachers in a passive-aggressive approach to gaining attention.

SOCIAL   Adolescents may be lazy because they hang out with friends who are lazy. They may simply be following the norms of the peer group.

What to Do

- Remember that a student who is lazy is behaving in this manner for some reason; no student wishes to fail. Laziness has definite roots that need to be explored.

- Ask the school psychologist to determine whether there are any particular circumstances underlying the student's laziness.
- Laziness may conceal a lack of confidence. If this appears to be the case, help the student build confidence gradually. This student needs a foundation of successful experiences, as well as appropriate social tools, to be an active participant in the classroom.
- Meet with the student privately in a comfortable setting. Explain that you are aware of his difficulty and want to help.
- Involve the student in different types of small-group activities so that he has the opportunity to work with all the members of his class. Assign these groups and monitor the interactions to ensure protection and success.
- Consult with the school counseling or social work staff or the school psychologist about including the student in a social skills group.
- If necessary, confer with the school's pupil personnel team.

Listening Difficulties

Why Students
May Exhibit This Behavior

ACADEMIC Students who are bored with academic subjects may tune out, daydream, or lose focus. At these times, they will probably not be listening to the teacher.

ENVIRONMENTAL Some adolescents may not listen to the teacher because they are preoccupied with problems on the home front. Others habitually do not listen to their parents, and they carry that attitude into school.

INTELLECTUAL Students with limited intellectual abilities may have trouble focusing and concentrating, and these difficulties can make them appear inattentive.

LINGUISTIC Students with language comprehension problems may not listen in the classroom simply because they do not understand what is being said or know how to respond.

MEDICAL Students with auditory problems will most likely exhibit difficulties in listening. Inattention is also one of the hallmark signs of attention deficit/hyperactivity disorder (AD/HD).

PERCEPTUAL Students who have auditory discrimination problems may not hear things the way others do. Eventually, after multiple experiences of failure, they give up and stop listening altogether.

PSYCHOLOGICAL Students suffering from depression, anxiety, or low self-esteem may be so consumed with their own psychological problems that listening to others is almost impossible.

SOCIAL Some students do not listen to the teacher because they are paying attention to what others are saying. These students are preoccupied with their social lives and do not give high priority to academic discussions and lectures.

What to Do

- Confer with the parents to convey your concern and find out whether the student's hearing needs to be checked.

- Ask the school psychologist if there are any circumstances that might be creating tension that could interfere with the student's ability to listen.

- Ask the speech/language therapist to screen the student. Even though the student's hearing may be fine, she may have other auditory processing problems.

- If the student's inability to listen appears based on oppositionality and defiance rather than on some other problem, establish and apply reinforcers and penalties for listening or not listening.

- Move the student to the front of the classroom to reduce extraneous stimuli and increase her chances of listening to you.

- Stand in front of the student whenever you have something important to say. Maintain a clear visual path from you to the student so that she can both see and hear what you are saying.

- If the problem is severe and persists, consult with the school's counseling or social work staff, the school psychologist, or the pupil personnel team.

Lying

Why Students May Exhibit This Behavior

ACADEMIC   Lying is often a cover-up for academic insecurity. Students who fear being seen as academically inadequate by their teachers or, more importantly, by their peers may make excuses and lie to protect their fragile egos.

ENVIRONMENTAL   Some students lie to avoid anticipated negative parental reactions sometimes associated with very high expectations, abuse, comparison or competition with siblings, and so on.

INTELLECTUAL   See *Academic.*

LINGUISTIC   See *Academic.*

PERCEPTUAL   See *Academic.*

PSYCHOLOGICAL   Some students may lie impulsively, out of anxiety, to avoid immediate negative reactions. They do not consider consequences but may feel guilt afterward. In other, more serious cases, students cannot differentiate between lies and reality, and they truly believe in what they say even though reality presents a very different picture.

SOCIAL   Students may lie to gain status within a social group. Feeling inadequate or insignificant and wanting to be accepted, they may fabricate or exaggerate information about their lives (e.g., parents' occupations, economic status, travels, experiences, possessions).

What to Do

- Before taking any action, obtain complete information about the situation so that you do not jump to conclusions or make false accusations.

- If you believe that the student has lied, speak with him privately to avoid embarrassing him. Addressing the situation in front of other students or adults will invite further lying because he will not want to be publicly humiliated.

- If you are reasonably sure that the student has lied, do not use entrapment—do not try to trick the student into admitting that he has lied.

- Be diplomatic, direct, and clear in confronting the student with the facts as you know them. Stay calm, but be firm to show that you are serious.

- After explaining your point of view, ask the student if he wants to rethink what he said. Don't pressure him if he does not respond immediately. Rather, say, "We will talk about this again some time today when you are ready, but we will definitely talk about it today."

- If the student admits to lying, say that you appreciate his honesty, then tell him what the consequences of the behavior will be. These should be appropriate and predetermined.

- If, in spite of overwhelming evidence, the student does not admit to lying, you must act on the evidence. Tell the student that the evidence indicates he did in fact lie and that he has violated class rules, then administer the consequences.

Lack of Motivation

Why Students
May Exhibit This Behavior

ACADEMIC   Students often have great difficulty motivating themselves to do academic work when they find the assignments boring, for whatever reason.

ENVIRONMENTAL   Some adolescents lack motivation in school because they face many problems at home, ranging from simple household disorganization to a nasty divorce battle or even neglect or abuse. These conflicts exert a more powerful pull than academic subjects.

INTELLECTUAL   Students with limited intelligence may lack motivation in school. On the other hand, gifted students may also have great difficulty with motivation because they rapidly become bored in a classroom designed for average students.

LINGUISTIC   Students who have difficulty understanding the language of instruction may have trouble keeping pace in the classroom. They can rapidly become frustrated and give up, losing all motivation in the process.

MEDICAL   Adolescents facing serious medical problems may lack motivation in school not because they find academics boring but rather because they are focused on their medical conditions.

PERCEPTUAL   Students who do not see the world as others do can experience great frustration in attempting to handle academic work. Eventually, the frustration can become overwhelming, and they are drained of motivation.

PSYCHOLOGICAL   Students who suffer from anxiety or depression may have no motivation in school. When life is not going well for them, they may lack the energy to engage in academic work.

SOCIAL   Some adolescents lack motivation for schoolwork because they are preoccupied with their social lives. They are capable of doing well academically, but they let social issues take precedence over assignments.

What to Do

- Remember that a student who exhibits lack of motivation is behaving in this manner for some reason. Because level of motivation is a direct function of available energy, lack of motivation indicates some energy drain that needs to be explored. Attempting to force the student into engagement may only create conflict, anxiety, and tension.

- Ask the school psychologist whether there are any particular circumstances underlying the student's lack of motivation.

- Help the student build confidence gradually. The unmotivated student needs a foundation of successful experiences, as well as social tools, in order to be an active participant in the classroom.

- Meet with the student privately in a comfortable setting. Explain that you are aware of her difficulty with motivation and that you want to help.

- Consult with the school counseling or social work staff or the school psychologist about including the student in a social skills group.

- If the problem is severe or persists, consult the school's pupil personnel team.

Writing and Passing Notes

Why Students
May Exhibit This Behavior

ACADEMIC   Some students write and pass notes in class out of simple boredom with the academic subject matter.

ENVIRONMENTAL   Although nearly all adolescents pass notes in class from time to time, parents need to remind them that such behavior is not acceptable. If parents do not reinforce understanding of appropriate schoolroom etiquette, adolescents may feel that it is acceptable to pass notes.

INTELLECTUAL   Students with limited intelligence may pass notes to classmates because they cannot understand what is going on in class. On the other hand, students with high intelligence may pass notes because they are bored with class work and occupy their extra time by communicating with classmates.

LINGUISTIC   Students with language problems may pass notes to elicit help, asking questions like "What is she saying?" "What does this mean?" or "I don't understand the teacher."

PERCEPTUAL   See *Linguistic*.

PSYCHOLOGICAL   Passing notes normally does not indicate a serious psychological problem, though it may embody some underlying messages regarding motives. Some students have a need to defy authority in a way that is not too dangerous. Others need to communicate about their emotions—for instance, young heartaches or crushes.

SOCIAL   The most common motive for passing notes in class is social communication at moments when students feel a strong need to talk but are not allowed to. The writing and passing of notes is a form of social bonding.

What to Do

- The writing and passing of notes is to be expected in an elementary classroom. Therefore, at the beginning of the school year, you should determine your policy regarding this behavior.

- On the first day of school, speak to the class about your policy on writing and passing notes. Explain why this behavior is inappropriate. Be sure the students understand what will happen if they are caught writing or passing notes.

- If a particular student habitually writes and passes notes, take the following measures:

  1. Seat the student in the front of the room near you so that you can better supervise him.

  2. Let the student have more interaction with classmates throughout the day so that he will not need to write notes to communicate with them.

  3. Plan many structured group activities to keep the student involved with classmates in appropriate ways.

  4. Speak privately with the student. Ask him why he habitually passes notes and whether he believes he can stop. Be fair but firm.

  5. Praise the student when you see him working on topics or projects that you know are completely school related. Let him know at that time that you recognize and are pleased with his work habits.

Nurse Visits

Why Students
May Exhibit This Behavior

ACADEMIC   Students who feel under intense academic pressure, either because they do not understand the subject matter or because they simply feel overwhelmed, may use visits to the nurse to relieve pressure or to avoid failure, embarrassment, or negative reactions from others.

ENVIRONMENTAL   Students who suffer separation anxiety may frequently visit the nurse in hopes of being sent home. Other students may visit the nurse on a regular basis in search of nurturance and attention they do not get at home.

INTELLECTUAL   See *Academic.*

LINGUISTIC   See *Academic.*

MEDICAL   Frequent visits to the nurse may be due to a variety of medical reasons, which should always be considered before other factors are examined.

PERCEPTUAL   See *Academic.*

PSYCHOLOGICAL   Some students visit the nurse frequently in search of nurturance, attention, recognition, or stability. They are attempting to relieve the tension of unmet needs. If this pattern is reinforced, the frequency of visits may increase.

SOCIAL   Students who experience social stress or rejection may visit the nurse during recess, lunch, or free time, when the chances of social interaction—and the fear of rejection—are greatest.

What to Do

Because frequent visits to the nurse may indicate an underlying medical problem, we strongly recommend that you immediately consult with the school nurse, the school psychologist, and/or the principal for reasons concerning the student's safety, your liability, the school's liability, and the parents' rights.

Lack of Organization

ACADEMIC Preoccupation with academic performance or fear of failure may cause a student to focus all available attention and energy in a single area. This sometimes results in disorganization and a lack of awareness of the requirements in other areas.

ENVIRONMENTAL An adolescent's disorganization may reflect a chaotic home environment or a lax parenting style that does not offer routines, boundaries, or systematic consequences.

INTELLECTUAL Students with limited intellectual ability may be disorganized because they feel overwhelmed, are unable to keep up with academic work, and do not adequately understand cause-and-effect relationships.

LINGUISTIC Language limitations that interfere with understanding of directions, nuances, and so forth may lead to internal and external disorganization.

MEDICAL Students with attention deficit/hyperactivity disorder (AD/HD) will have a very difficult time being consistently organized. The variables exhibited by this disorder include impulsivity, distractibility, inattention, and disorganization.

PERCEPTUAL Disorganization may be the result of perceptual limitations because organization requires the harmonious working of internal and external systems.

PSYCHOLOGICAL Extreme tension or anxiety may create a "fog" in a student that may impair his understanding of the implications of his actions. When this occurs, organization, which requires awareness of consequences and internal energy, falters. External disorganization in this case is reflective of the internal disorganization the student feels as a result of the tension.

SOCIAL   Preoccupation with social concerns may drain away the energy that a student needs for many other school-related purposes, including maintaining some sort of organization.

What to Do

- Speak privately with the student. Ask why he thinks he is having problems with organization, and ask him directly how you can be of assistance.
- Stress the importance of organization to the student. Explain why it is critical for academic success.
- Teach the student how to be organized. Show him how to put things in their proper places.
- Provide the student with organizational tools (a container for pencils and pens, a box for homework papers, etc.).
- Give the student time at the beginning and at the end of the day to organize his materials so that he starts and finishes the day on a positive note.
- After each assignment is done, check the student's organization of it so he never falls too far behind and becomes completely disorganized.
- Have the student write down all the materials needed for a given assignment, especially in the case of homework. (He may need your help with this.)
- Set up a token economy/reward system to recognize good organizational practices.
- Teach the student to discard irrelevant and old papers and to store important ones. Many times, students have difficulty determining what to throw out and what to keep.
- Send a note home to the parents explaining what you are trying to accomplish. Offer suggestions for helping the student strengthen organizational skills at home.
- Disorganization is a sign of a possible learning disability. Therefore, if the problem is severe and persists, you should consult with the school counseling or social work staff, the school psychologist, or the pupil personnel team.

Overreactivity

Why Students
May Exhibit This Behavior

ACADEMIC   Serious and consistent academic pressure and fear of failure may cause a student to overreact, especially with peers.

ENVIRONMENTAL   Family difficulties, struggles, dysfunction, arguments, pressures, and so on may all conspire to drain an adolescent's energy. Patience, which is based on available energy, suffers, and overreactions occur.

LINGUISTIC   In students who have language difficulties, over-reactions may stem from perceived or real feelings of not being understood or of being ridiculed.

PERCEPTUAL   Misperception of social cues is common in some students with perceptual disorders. Overreaction to situations may result.

PSYCHOLOGICAL   Overreaction is, in many students, the result of pent-up frustration, anger, confusion, or fear. Like air in an over-inflated balloon, the tension from such issues builds and may explode in response to a minimally stressful situation or comment. Other students may have psychological disorders that are manifested in frequent overreaction. Some conditions, such as conduct disorder or oppositional defiant disorder, may require professional intervention. Overreactions associated with these disorders can be intense, violent, and consistent, and may be directed toward both peers and authority figures.

- Oppositional defiant disorder, the less serious of the two, is usually characterized by patterns of negative, hostile, and defiant behaviors with peers and adults. These behaviors may include swearing and frequent episodes of intense anger and annoyance. The behaviors associated with oppositional defiant disorder usually appear around age 8, generally not later than early adolescence. In the classroom, students with this disorder may exhibit low frustration tolerance, frequent temper outbursts, low self-confidence, unwillingness to take responsibility for their actions, and consistent blaming of others for their own mistakes or problems.

- Conduct disorder is characterized by a persistent pattern of intrusive behavior that violates the basic rights of others and shows no concern for implications or consequences. This pattern is not selective and is exhibited in the home, at school, with the student's peers, and in the community. This condition may also manifest itself in vandalism, stealing, physical aggression, cruelty to animals, or fire setting. In school, conduct-disordered students may be physically confrontational with teachers and peers, have poor attendance, and exhibit other forms of antisocial behavior. Moreover, they may frequently be suspended, thereby missing a great deal of academic work.

SOCIAL Overreaction may stem from a need to be in control, a desire for the spotlight, or a feeling of social devaluation. Some students overreact in dramatic ways to gain social attention or to be perceived as victims, in either case to meet a need for recognition. If such behavior is reinforced, the student learns to perpetuate and refine it.

What to Do

- Try to determine what, exactly, is making the student overreact. With many students, it is a specific individual, event, or task.
- Speak privately with the student and discuss what you have observed. Ask her to explain why she overreacts so often.
- After listening to the student, do what you can to make the necessary changes in the classroom so that she can function more easily.
- Seat the student at the front of the classroom so that you can better supervise her and prevent overreactive behavior from developing.
- If the student cannot maintain self-control, remove her from the environment for the safety of the other students.

- If necessary, contact the parents to see if any circumstances at home may be causing the student to overreact.
- Let the student know that she can opt out of an activity if she feels frustration, anger, and the like coming on. Devise an acceptable way for the student to deal with this situation and a signal she can give you when she feels tension building.
- Seat the student next to another student who you know will not arouse anger or hostility in her.
- Consult with the school counseling or social work staff or the school psychologist about the possibility of helping the student develop better coping skills or setting up a behavior modification program for the student.
- If the problem is severe and persists, consult with the school's pupil personnel team.

Panic

Why Students
May Exhibit This Behavior

ACADEMIC   Students who fear parental reactions, embarrassment before peers, and so on may panic in academic situations. Also, students who feel unprepared or who have histories of failure and anticipate more failure may panic easily in these situations.

ENVIRONMENTAL   Students whose parents do not provide boundaries, protection, direction, consistency, or logical consequences may tend to panic. Students who do not feel well protected by parents who themselves may be vulnerable, uninvolved, or self-absorbed may fear that any situation could lead to harm or danger. They see themselves as alone in dealing with the world, and they spend much of their available energy on self-protection.

INTELLECTUAL   Students with low intellectual ability may panic easily as a result of feeling overwhelmed and lost.

LINGUISTIC   See *Intellectual.*

PERCEPTUAL   See *Intellectual.*

PSYCHOLOGICAL   Students who do not feel a secure protective barrier between themselves and the outside world will panic easily out of a sense of vulnerability. These students may lack self-esteem or social tools, or they may have experienced trauma or environmental influences that make them vulnerable. Also, students with high levels of tension may panic easily because they are drained of the energy required to maintain perspective.

SOCIAL   In some students, the need for social connection is so strong that any real or perceived social isolation or rejection may cause them to panic and, in consequence, to misperceive the actions of others.

What to Do

- Remember that a student who panics easily feels very unsure of himself and his situation. Therefore, attempting to force him into particular situations will only create tremendous conflict, anxiety, and tension.

- Ask the school psychologist whether there are any external circumstances underlying the student's panic.

- Speak with the student privately in a comfortable setting. Explain that you are aware of his difficulty and that you want to help.

- Try to help the student feel more comfortable in the classroom. At times, this may be like coaxing a frightened turtle out of its shell. It requires patience.

- Help the student build confidence over time. The student who panics needs a foundation of successful experiences, as well as the appropriate social tools, to be an active participant in the classroom.

- Have the student work in groups so that he can build confidence in the classroom. Have the groups work on simple goal-oriented tasks that will give the student the feeling of belonging and group accomplishment.

- Provide a variety of small-group activities so that the student has the opportunity to work with all the members of his class. Assign groups and monitor interactions to ensure protection and success.

- Consult with the school counseling or social work staff or the school psychologist about the possibility of including the student in a social skills group or setting up a behavior modification program for him.

- If the problem is severe and persists, consult with the school's pupil personnel team.

Lack of Participation

Why Students
May Exhibit This Behavior

ACADEMIC   Some students have great difficulty participating in things that they do not enjoy. If these things include academics, the students will not express interest in any academic independent or group assignment.

ENVIRONMENTAL   Some adolescents fail to participate in class because of problems at home, ranging from household disorganization to a nasty divorce battle or possible neglect or abuse. To avoid dealing with the pain of the home circumstances, these students simply keep to themselves.

INTELLECTUAL   For some students, limited intelligence can hinder involvement in class. On the other hand, students with very high intelligence may fail to participate in activities because they rapidly become bored in a classroom designed for average students.

LINGUISTIC   When a student has difficulty understanding the language of instruction, she can rapidly become frustrated and give up. This leads to a reluctance to participate because the student fears teasing and ridicule from peers. It becomes safer just to keep quiet and hope that the teacher does not call on her.

MEDICAL   For some students, medical problems may interfere with participation in classroom activities. For example, a student with asthma may not join in because she is having trouble breathing. A student in a wheelchair may decline to participate because he finds the logistics too complicated.

PERCEPTUAL   Students who do not see the world as others do can encounter great frustration in trying to participate in class activities. They repeatedly experience failure and eventually give up.

PSYCHOLOGICAL   Depression and anxiety keep some students from participating in class activities. If they are worried or scared about events or circumstances in their lives, they may not have the mental energy to do what others are doing.

SOCIAL   Some students are not involved in classroom activities because they are never chosen for teams or groups. In a sense, they are viewed as outcasts by their peers. As hard as the teacher may try to integrate them with others, they just do not fit in. Eventually, they lose the desire to participate because it is embarrassing or ego deflating.

What to Do

- Remember that a student who refrains from participating in classroom activities is doing so for some protective reason. Therefore, attempting to force her into an activity will only create tremendous conflict, anxiety, and tension.

- Ask the school psychologist whether there are any external circumstances underlying the lack of participation.

- Speak privately with the student in a comfortable setting. Explain that you are aware of her difficulty with participation and that you want to help.

- Help the student feel more comfortable in the classroom. At times, this may be like coaxing a frightened turtle out of its shell. It requires patience.

- Help the student build confidence over time. The student who does not participate needs a foundation of successful experiences, as well as the appropriate social tools, to become active in the classroom.

- Provide practical guidance and support. For instance, involve the student in small groups and then, if appropriate, gradually increase the size of the groups. Initially, group her with classmates you know are sensitive to others' feelings.

- Have the groups work on simple goal-oriented tasks that will give the student the feeling of belonging and group accomplishment. Assign groups and monitor interactions to ensure protection and success.

- Provide a variety of small-group activities so that the student has the opportunity to work with all the members of her class.

- Consult with the school counseling or social work staff or the school psychologist about having the student join a social skills group.
- If lack of participation is extreme or persists, consult the school's pupil personnel team.

Excessive Pleasing Behavior

Why Students
May Exhibit This Behavior

ACADEMIC   Many students use academic success or accomplishment to get recognition or validation from the teacher. Although this is not uncommon, the frequency, intensity, and duration of the approval-seeking behavior distinguish the normal from the anxiety driven.

ENVIRONMENTAL   An adolescent who needs to please all the time may have parents who send inconsistent messages of love and validation. Such parents change moods and rules frequently and are inconsistent in showing love and affection. The student never learns a frame of reference and hence has an obsessive need to please.

INTELLECTUAL   See *Perceptual*.

LINGUISTIC   See *Academic*.

PERCEPTUAL   A student with perceptual deficits may misperceive or distort the meanings of the teacher's facial expressions, verbal directives, comments, and so on. In doing so, the student may write a script that creates anxiety. In order to reduce this anxiety, the student tries excessively to please the teacher.

PSYCHOLOGICAL   The absence of feelings of validation, love, nurturance, caring, approval, significance, and so on may underlie the excessive need to please the teacher. If the timing is appropriate and the student's effort seems to be logical, then the attempt to please may not be a problem. However, if it seems illogical, poorly timed, impulsive, and so on, then the motive should be of concern.

What to Do

Normally, an effort to please the teacher is usually a healthy direction for a student's energy. However, you will need to determine whether or not the student is excessively needy. If the frequency, intensity, and duration of the behavior suggest that it may be neurotically motivated, refer to the sections on need for immediate attention and attention seeking.

High Popularity

ACADEMIC   Popularity is often related directly to grades. Some students' outstanding school performance elicits the admiration of their peers. Classmates want to work on group projects with them and even receive tutoring from them.

ENVIRONMENTAL   Popularity is reflected onto some adolescents by older siblings. A student who has a brother or sister who is popular in the school may also become popular simply because of this connection. Other adolescents are popular because their parents nurture their self-confidence and self-esteem: Adolescents who believe in themselves are more likely to be popular.

INTELLECTUAL   See *Academic.*

LINGUISTIC   For some students, popularity comes from an ability to communicate ideas effectively. The classic example is leadership in student government.

MEDICAL   Some students may be popular by virtue of physical characteristics. A boy may be popular because his size and strength enable him to excel in sports. An example of unwelcome popularity is the young girl who reaches puberty earlier than most of her peers: She is sought after by boys, but in a negative way.

PSYCHOLOGICAL   Some students are popular because they believe in themselves. They have great inner strength for their age and enjoy being in the spotlight. Their confidence and feelings of security enable them to stand up and lead others.

SOCIAL   Adolescents who are engaged in many social activities—athletics, chess club, chorus, band, and the like—become popular because they are involved with so many people in a variety of settings.

What to Do

Although a student's popularity generally will not be of concern for teachers, there are times when popular students do not effectively balance schoolwork and social life. Excessive investment in social interactions can impair academic performance and success. If, in a popular student, you see inconsistency, defying authority, clowning, procrastination, or other specific problems, we recommend that you refer to the appropriate sections in this book.

Low Popularity

Why Students
May Exhibit This Behavior

ACADEMIC   Some students are not accepted because they are either too bright or too "dumb" in the eyes of their peers. A student who differs from others academically can pose a threat to classmates' egos. On the one hand, students may avoid a gifted student because she may be labeled a "geek" or a "nerd." On the other hand, associating with a student considered "stupid" can be thought of as a reflection on oneself.

ENVIRONMENTAL   Unfortunately, many students tend to be very superficial and to base their likes and dislikes on where people live and what they have. For instance, a student with limited economic circumstances may not be accepted by more affluent classmates because she does not have the things that they do.

INTELLECTUAL   See *Academic.*

LINGUISTIC   Some students may not be accepted because they have accents or do not speak clearly. Classmates may fear being ostracized by their peers if they are friendly toward a student who speaks differently.

MEDICAL   Some students may be not be accepted by their peers for reasons of size or development. A boy may be unaccepted because he is much smaller than his peers and cannot do well in sports. A girl who experiences early puberty—and consequently attracts male attention—may find herself alienated from her female peers.

PSYCHOLOGICAL   Some students do not gain acceptance from their peers because they do not believe in themselves. They have little inner strength for their age and tend to avoid the spotlight. Their low confidence and expressions of insecurity can be aversive to others.

SOCIAL   Some students are not involved in any social activities, with the result that others do not get to know them. Their lack of acceptance stems from anonymity and lack of contact with peers.

What to Do

- Speak privately with the student. Ask why she feels she is not popular with her peers and how she feels about the situation.
- Discuss the importance of friendship. Teach the student some coping skills to help her make friends with her classmates.
- Plan more group activities so that students get more chances to interact.
- Reward teamwork within the class.
- Speak with the student's parents. Find out if the student can become more involved in extracurricular activities.
- Consult with the school counseling or social work staff or the school psychologist about the possibility of including the student in a social skills group.
- If the problem is severe and persists, consult with the school's pupil personnel team.

Procrastination

ACADEMIC   Students procrastinate in academic situations in attempts to delay anticipated failure, negative reaction, or embarrassment, or to avoid confronting the reality that they do not know what they are doing.

ENVIRONMENTAL   Procrastination as a coping mechanism is often seen in families where violence or other forms of abuse are common. In other homes, students may procrastinate to get back at parents who are controlling or who may have overly high expectations. In this case, procrastination is an attempt to avoid negative reaction, loss of status in the family, and parental disappointment.

INTELLECTUAL   See *Academic.*

LINGUISTIC   See *Academic.*

PERCEPTUAL   Students with perceptual deficits may use procrastination as a means of dealing with situations that they do not fully understand. Because the variables and nuances necessary for appropriate responses elude them, they procrastinate to avoid negative consequences.

PSYCHOLOGICAL   For some students, procrastination may be an effort to exercise control over their environments or others. Holding back may offer them the only power they feel in their lives. Other students procrastinate to defer a reality with which they feel unprepared to cope. Still others may procrastinate to avoid anticipated negative reactions from significant individuals in their lives.

SOCIAL   Procrastination may stem from fear of negative social response, rejection, devaluation, or embarrassment. It should be distinguished from delay: Procrastination may be perpetual, whereas delay lasts a short while before the individual deals with the situation. When a student procrastinates, other students lose patience, further compounding the student's fears.

What to Do

A pattern of procrastination will have adverse effects on a student's educational success. This pattern should not be allowed to continue once observed. It is imperative that you try to identify the causes of the student's need to procrastinate. Then refer to the sections in this book that address laziness, lack of interest in school, and failure to complete homework.

Excessive Questions

Why Students
May Exhibit This Behavior

ACADEMIC Academic confusion resulting from learning disabilities, academic anxiety, concrete thinking, difficulty with abstract concepts, and so on may motivate some students to ask questions constantly. However, other students with the same factors may withdraw and never ask any questions.

ENVIRONMENTAL Excessive questioning can stem from various environmental causes. Some adolescents come from homes where questions are encouraged and curiosity is fostered. If the questions are higher level and used to satisfy curiosity or resolve confusion, then this may be the case. However, if the questions are disconnected, basic, concrete, repetitive, and so on, then the underlying cause may be different. In this case, the student may be motivated by emptiness and a lack of parental intervention or attention. Another possible motive for constant questioning is to maintain a captive audience, one that may not be available at home.

INTELLECTUAL Students with limited intellectual ability and concrete thinking patterns may easily become confused by directions of any kind and may resort to constant questions because they are lost.

LINGUISTIC Students with receptive language disorders and bilingual students who may need constant clarification or assistance with language and word labels may ask questions continually.

PERCEPTUAL Some students with processing problems ask many questions in attempts to buy time. They tend to become anxious about their slow pace and resort to repeated questions to prevent discomfort in other people. Other students with processing deficits ask many questions because they cannot grasp the concepts and try many avenues to comprehend and gain more information.

Psychological   Some students are in great need of attention and utilize constant questions to stay in the spotlight. Other students ask many questions because their anxiety levels are so high that they cannot retain information, especially in tasks involving short-term memory.

Social   Some students ask questions constantly in attempts to gain social status and recognition.

What to Do

- Speak privately with the student about what you are observing. Explain that although you appreciate his interest, his questions are becoming excessive and need to be limited.

- Let the student explain his side of the story. It is very important to find out why he asks questions constantly. Is it because he does not understand assignments, needs excessive attention, and so on?

- Get involved with the student as much as possible to limit the potential for excessive questions.

- If the student has intellectual limitations, consider simplifying directions and other presentations.

- Seat the student next to a peer who can help him out and who may be able to answer his questions.

- Let the student participate as much as possible in class discussions so that he feels that he is getting the attention he needs.

- Contact the parents if the situation warrants it. Find out if excessive questioning is a behavior specific to school or occurs at home as well.

- When the excessive questioning begins, be sure to act immediately to let the student know that the behavior is not acceptable.

- When the student refrains from asking many questions and works independently, praise him for his appropriate behavior.

- If necessary, consult with the school counseling or social work staff or the school psychologist about the possibility of setting up a behavior modification program for the student.

- If the problem is severe and persists, consult with the school's pupil personnel team.

Risky Behavior

Why Students
May Exhibit This Behavior

ACADEMIC   Years of academic failure coupled with parental rejection or disappointment could result in a student's turning to risky behavior. Hurting oneself is the ultimate expression of anger toward parents in some cases.

ENVIRONMENTAL   Adolescents from homes characterized by abusive, chaotic, irrational, violent, or questionable parenting styles may resort to all types of risky behavior patterns. These patterns arise from self-doubt, self-hatred, depression, feelings of entrapment, loss of hope, anger turned inward, or the need to embarrass or inspire regret in their parents.

INTELLECTUAL   Students with limited intellectual ability may not be aware that their behavior is risky because they may lack abstract reasoning ability, mature social skills, or understanding of cause-and-effect relationships.

MEDICAL   Risky behavior can often be seen in students with severe attention deficit/hyperactivity disorder (AD/HD). Their impulsivity is so automatic that they simply do not think about consequences.

PSYCHOLOGICAL   Risky behavior is often a cry for help. An adolescent who attempts high-risk actions may feel desperately unloved, uncared for, or lost. Her need is for someone to recognize her situation and take care of her. However, such behavior is often misread, ignored, overreacted to, or rationalized as "kids will be kids." When this occurs, the intensity and frequency of risky behavior escalate as the cry for help goes unheeded. Risky behavior may also be a pattern for students who are impulsive, difficult, rambunctious, and immature, and who do not understand the consequences of their behavior. These students are often characterized by parents as having had behavior problems very early.

SOCIAL   Certain students may engage in risky behavior in attempts to gain social recognition, become part of a group that thrives on such behavior, keep up with peers, or show off for someone of the opposite sex.

What to Do

If you observe risky behavior, we strongly recommend that you immediately consult with the school psychologist and/or the principal for reasons concerning the student's safety, your liability, the school's liability, and the parents' rights.

Difficulty Remaining Seated

Why Students
May Exhibit This Behavior

ACADEMIC Frustration is probably the most common academic reason students cannot remain in their seats. When they are confronted with work for which they feel inadequate, any avoidance is better than sitting. Getting up to get a drink, visit the bathroom, throw out papers, ask the teacher some trivial question, and the like may all be maneuvers to avoid ego-deflating academic situations.

ENVIRONMENTAL Adolescents from homes where limits and guidelines are lax may feel that they can do whatever they like at any time. Such adolescents have not yet incorporated the internal controls that are usually developed through parenting that provides fair but consistent boundaries and appropriate consequences for behaviors.

INTELLECTUAL Students with limited intellectual ability may lose interest quickly and need to move around to ease their frustrations.

MEDICAL Students who are always moving and have difficulty remaining in their seats may have attention deficit/hyperactivity disorder (AD/HD). Students who have vision problems may get up to see what is on the board. Also, some students may be on medications whose side effects include impulsivity and heightened activity.

PERCEPTUAL Students who have temporal or spatial organizational difficulties may not perceive the problems caused by moving about frequently.

PSYCHOLOGICAL Students with very high levels of internal or nervous tension may not be able to sit still for long periods. When the tension gets too high, it drains the capacities for patience, focus, ability to attend, concentration, and judgment.

SOCIAL   Some students may leave their seats constantly to visit friends, walk past classmates they like or want to antagonize, pass notes, seek reassurance, or get attention.

What to Do

- Ask the school psychologist whether the student has been diagnosed with AD/HD or has ever received special education services.

- Ask the school nurse whether the student is on any medication for hyperactivity (e.g., Ritalin).

- If the answers to the foregoing questions are negative, speak privately with the student. Ask him why he cannot remain seated. Many students who move about constantly are either bored or seeking attention.

- Clarify the class rules to the student and explain the difference between appropriate and inappropriate behavior. It is possible that the student has not experienced the type of structure necessary for success at his grade level.

- Because students with high activity levels often have great difficulty remaining seated, it is imperative that you plan ahead for this behavior. You should decide what to do if the behavior affects the class and then administer the appropriate consequences.

- If the situation is seriously affecting the student's social, emotional, or academic functioning, confer with the parents. However, do not discuss the idea of medication with the parents. Even if you think medication is appropriate, this is not your role nor your area of expertise.

- If necessary, consult with the school counseling or social work staff or the school psychologist.

- If the problem is severe and persists, consult with the school's pupil personnel team.

Shyness

ACADEMIC   Poor academic ability may make a student feel inadequate and result in low self-esteem and verbal hesitancy that may be construed as shyness.

ENVIRONMENTAL   Some adolescents may be shy because they have overly critical parents or because they are subject to verbal or physical abuse. Their shyness is a way to avoid stirring up problems by saying or doing the wrong thing. In other cases, students are shy as a result of family patterns of shyness and behavior modeled at home.

INTELLECTUAL   Students with intellectual limitations may lack confidence in speaking, especially if they have received negative responses as a result of their limitations.

LINGUISTIC   Certain types of language disorders or articulation problems (i.e., lisps, immature speech patterns) may make students unwilling to communicate for fear of negative reactions.

MEDICAL   Certain types of organic speech disorders can affect a student's ability or willingness to interact with peers.

PERCEPTUAL   Certain processing problems (i.e., auditory expressive problems) may interfere with a student's ability to track conversations or respond in a timely fashion. Peer reactions to these problems may limit the student's willingness to interact.

PSYCHOLOGICAL   In some students, severe anxiety and tension can be misinterpreted as shyness because they lead to preoccupation and self-absorption. In other cases, shyness may be the result of depression or—in extreme cases—selective mutism, characterized by a refusal to speak in social or school situations despite adequate intelligence and language development.

SOCIAL Students may be shy because they fear rejection by peers, lack confidence in social situations, have poor social skills, fear being victimized by others, or do not understand social rules and norms.

What to Do

- Remember that shyness fulfills some protective function. Therefore, attempting to force a shy student into a social situation will only create tremendous conflict, anxiety, and tension.
- Ask the school psychologist whether there are any external circumstances underlying the student's shyness.
- To encourage the shy student to open up, help her feel comfortable in the classroom. At times, this may be like coaxing a frightened turtle out of its shell. It requires patience.
- Speak privately with the student in a comfortable setting. Explain that you are aware of her difficulty in social situations and that you want to help.
- Help the student build confidence gradually. The shy student needs a foundation of successful experiences, as well as the appropriate social tools, to be an active participant in the classroom.
- Provide practical guidance. For instance, involve the shy student in small groups and then, if appropriate, gradually increase the group size. Initially, group the student with others who you know are more sensitive.
- Have the group work on simple goal-oriented tasks that will give the student the feeling of belonging and group accomplishment.
- Provide a variety of small-group activities so that the student has the opportunity to work with all the members of her class. Assign these groups and monitor the interactions to ensure protection and success.
- Consult with the school counseling or social work staff or the school psychologist about having the student join a social skills group.
- If the problem is severe or persists, confer with the school's pupil personnel team.

Slow Starting

Why Students
May Exhibit This Behavior

ACADEMIC   Academic avoidance, fear of failure, a lack of conceptual understanding, and so on may all lead to a student's being a slow starter. Further, students who have experienced lags in learning may also need more time to get started because they may not have full mastery of the concepts.

ENVIRONMENTAL   Adolescents who are preoccupied with family stress, dysfunction, and so on may not have the resources available to focus on and attend to tasks. Further, adolescents from homes where academic motivation is not emphasized may lack a desire for schoolwork.

INTELLECTUAL   Intellectually limited students may have difficulty starting work because they may take longer to grasp ideas, concepts, and directions, and may easily become confused.

LINGUISTIC   Students with language processing difficulties, especially concerning receptive language functions, may be slow to start work because they may not fully understand what is expected.

MEDICAL   Some medical conditions or medications may lead to low energy levels and less than normal activity.

PERCEPTUAL   Students with processing difficulties may appear to be procrastinating, whereas in reality they are having difficulty starting because they have slow processing speeds.

PSYCHOLOGICAL   Intense anxiety and tension can weigh a student down and interfere with the ability to concentrate, become organized, and get started.

What to Do

- Repeat and clarify the assignment and observe the student until he starts.

- If many students in the class appear to have the same problem, reevaluate the assignments for interest and motivational potential.

- Provide more gross motor activities and exercises before academic work to help the student wake up and get ready for the school day.

- Make sure that the student is aware of the time limits associated with assignments. Clarify what will happen if he does not get started and finish the work on time.

- Provide some type of incentive for the student to start work on time and do the work as everyone else does.

- Use gentle prompts throughout the early part of the day to motivate the student and remind him that you are watching him.

- If the problem is severe and persists, consult with the school counseling or social work staff, the school psychologist, or the pupil personnel team.

Smoking

Why Students
May Exhibit This Behavior

ENVIRONMENTAL   Adolescents who come from homes where parents smoke are more likely to smoke themselves. Other environmental factors contributing to adolescents' need to smoke include family tension, which creates anxiety. In this case, smoking reduces feelings of tension.

MEDICAL   Adolescents with serious illnesses may turn to smoking because they view it as one of the things in their lives that they can control. Once they start smoking, adolescents may continue as a result of nicotine addiction.

PSYCHOLOGICAL   Smoking is related to a number of psychological reasons. Most commonly, smoking gives adolescents a sense of being "grown up" and having a separate identity. It is a way to rebel that is not too rebellious (i.e., it does not have many legal consequences, nor is it looked on as being as serious as drug or alcohol use).

SOCIAL   Regardless of what the adolescent feels, peer influence is very compelling. If friends smoke, then a youngster is likely to take it up.

What to Do

Interventions at the classroom level may not be appropriate for smoking, although schoolwide anti-smoking policies and prevention programs can be quite helpful. Your best response is probably to give your full support to schoolwide efforts.

Squinting

Why Students
May Exhibit This Behavior

ACADEMIC   Squinting may be a manifestation of tension caused by academic stress, particularly if the stress is of long duration.

ENVIRONMENTAL   Adolescents suffering from stress at home may vent their tension through bodily movements, including squinting.

MEDICAL   Squinting may be caused by any number of eye problems that should be investigated immediately. Students with undetected eye problems often squint to compensate for poor vision.

PERCEPTUAL   See *Academic.*

PSYCHOLOGICAL   Squinting may have a psychological origin in such conditions as tic disorders, or it may be a release for nervous tension.

What to Do

Because squinting may have medical or psychological roots, we strongly recommend that you immediately consult with the school psychologist, the school nurse, and the principal for reasons concerning the student's safety, your liability, the school's liability, and the parents' rights.

Stealing

Why Students
May Exhibit This Behavior

ACADEMIC   Students experiencing academic frustration may displace it toward authority figures through destructive behaviors, stealing being a common example.

ENVIRONMENTAL   Adolescents who steal may see this behavior modeled by significant people in their lives, such as older siblings. They may become involved in stealing because they lack after-school supervision. Some adolescents may live in neighborhoods where stealing is viewed as acceptable.

INTELLECTUAL   Students with intellectual limitations may not understand the ramifications and consequences of stealing.

PSYCHOLOGICAL   Some students may steal as a way of displacing anger. They unconsciously derive satisfaction that they are not getting elsewhere in their lives. More often than not, they do not need the things they are stealing. Other students may steal because their overall moral judgment concerning acceptable behaviors is underdeveloped for their age.

SOCIAL   Some adolescents may steal because their friends are doing it, as when students go together into a store and one dares another to take something. They steal simply to be accepted.

What to Do

- Before taking action, obtain all possible information about the situation to avoid making false accusations.
- If you believe that a student has stolen, speak to her privately to avoid embarrassing her. If you address the situation in front of anyone, the student will be less likely to tell the truth because she will not want to be publicly humiliated.

- If you are reasonably sure that the student has stolen, do not use entrapment. Do not try to trick her.

- Be diplomatic, clear, and direct in confronting the student with the facts as you know them. Speak calmly, but be firm. Show the student that you are serious.

- After explaining your point of view, ask the student if she wants to rethink her actions. Don't pressure her to respond immediately. Rather, say, "We will talk about this again some time today when you are ready, but we will definitely talk about it today."

- If the student admits to stealing, thank her for her honesty, then tell her what the consequences of her behavior will be. The consequences should be predetermined and appropriate.

- If the student does not admit to stealing, you must act on the basis of the evidence. Tell the student that the evidence indicates that she did steal and violate class rules, then administer the consequences.

- If stealing is a consistent pattern of behavior, the problem is serious enough to warrant your consulting with parents, the counseling or social work staff, or the school psychologist. Referring the matter to the pupil personnel team may be appropriate.

Making Up Stories

Why Students
May Exhibit This Behavior

ACADEMIC Students who get poor grades may tend to lie about their performance, generally out of embarrassment. Academic failure can create anxiety about how they will be perceived by others, and they fabricate for emotional survival.

ENVIRONMENTAL Some parents pressure their students to "be the best." For most of these students, that will never be possible, yet it may be the only way to gain parental acceptance. When they do poorly in class or get in trouble, they fear severe negative reactions, and they fabricate stories that they think will please.

INTELLECTUAL See *Perceptual* and *Social*.

PERCEPTUAL Students with perceptual problems may have difficulty reading. To compensate, they may make up stories about what they have read because they were not able to read or comprehend the assigned work.

PSYCHOLOGICAL Some students have a psychological need to make up stories because it gives them a sense of power. For some, the stories are harmless attempts to show people how good they are. For others, the stories can be quite problematic. The stories turn into lies, and a need arises to keep lying because this is all the student knows.

SOCIAL Some students invent stories about their accomplishments and activities to gain peer approval. They may do so because they feel socially insecure and uncomfortable with themselves as they are.

What to Do

- Speak privately with the student. Discuss his possible reasons for making up stories.

- Determine whether the student's fabrications are harmful or simply the fruits of a good imagination. If it is just a case of imagination, you may be able to ignore the behavior unless it gets out of hand.

- If the student gives you a good explanation, accept it and explain why you want him to tell the truth.

- Invite the student to write creative stories to channel his imagination into constructive outlets.

- Praise the student for honesty and for telling the truth.

- Talk to the student about establishing a reputation with others. Explain that making up stories can be detrimental to his future reputation and to friendships.

- If the student denies making up stories, review the class rules concerning lying.

- Talk to the parents about the situation. It may be important to know whether this problem occurs only in school or forms a pattern in the student's home life as well.

- If the fabrications persist or escalate to a point where they constitute lying, see the section on lying in this book.

- If the problem persists to the point where the student seems to believe his own fabrications or appears unable to stop his behavior, consult with the school counseling or social work staff, the school psychologist, or the school's pupil personnel team.

Stubbornness

Why Students
May Exhibit This Behavior

ACADEMIC   Students who fear academic ridicule, failure, or peer reaction may be stubborn when it comes to academic assignments. Fear gives rise to an internal panic that may be exhibited through stubbornness.

ENVIRONMENTAL   Students whose parents have excessively high expectations, offer minimal boundaries and guidance, or are abusive may use stubbornness as a means of coping and avoiding negative reactions. Other students who are immature or infantalized (allowed to maintain immature styles and held back from becoming independent to satisfy parents' emotional needs) may be stubborn because of limited skill development.

INTELLECTUAL   A student with limited intellectual ability may be very rigid and concrete in her thinking and may consequently make decisions on issues without seeing the whole picture. Once having taken a position, she may lack the insight, ability, skills, or intellect to change it or see other options.

PSYCHOLOGICAL   High levels of tension drain away the energy required for patience, judgment, and appropriate responses. Students with this problem may stonewall or lock onto positions because they are unsure what to do, do not feel comfortable making choices or decisions, and so on. These students lack the ability to change positions diplomatically or appropriately. Instead, they hold their ground even though the facts might contradict them.

SOCIAL   Some students become stubborn when they do not get their way in social situations. Their stubbornness is an expression of anger.

What to Do

- Speak privately with the student. Keeping in mind that stubborn behavior is a sign not of strength but of a fragile ego, establish yourself as the benevolent authority.

- Explain to the student that you understand that she may have issues causing her to be stubborn and that you will help her try to understand them but that you will not tolerate this behavior.

- Stress the seriousness of the situation and the consequences if it continues.

- Try to help the student understand why she is being stubborn. Encourage her to verbalize what she is feeling or why she behaves as she does. If she cannot give voice to her feelings, you may want to provide some labels for what she may be feeling.

- Suggest to the student alternative means of resolving future conflicts. Many students who become stubborn know no other way to handle difficult and stressful situations.

- If stubbornness is a consistent pattern of behavior for the student, consult with the school counseling or social work staff or the school psychologist about the possibility of setting up a meeting with the parents and/or developing a behavioral contract for the student.

- If the problem is severe and persists, consult with the school's pupil personnel team.

Substance Abuse

Why Students
May Exhibit This Behavior

ACADEMIC Adolescents who experience continual academic failure may feel so depressed that they may turn to drugs or alcohol to numb these feelings and make them go away, at least temporarily.

ENVIRONMENTAL Adolescents who turn to drugs or alcohol may do so because of parental neglect or lack of supervision (interpreted by adolescents as not caring), family violence, dysfunction, or parental fears of confrontation and boundary setting.

MEDICAL Some students may become involved in substance abuse to self-medicate feelings of stress, tension, anxiety, or depression.

PSYCHOLOGICAL Reasons for this problem vary with the individual. Low self-esteem and lack of awareness of ways to relieve stress play a role. Drugs or alcohol become a "quick fix," and students soon become conditioned to believe in this way of dealing with problems.

SOCIAL The primary social reason for involvement with drugs and alcohol is peer influence and the adolescent's need to be accepted. Often social factors override the adolescent's personal beliefs about the use of these substances.

What to Do

Even if it is obvious that a student has been drinking or is on drugs, as a teacher you do not want to put yourself in the position of making accusations. If you suspect a student is high, consider sending him to the school nurse along with a message that the student does not seem well. The nurse can then briefly evaluate the student's medical condition, then contact the principal, dean of students, or parents so the student can be taken to the emergency room. If the student is not high but you suspect long-term use, notify an administrator and make a referral as soon as possible.

Suicidal Behavior

Why Students
May Exhibit This Behavior

ACADEMIC Some adolescents cannot succeed in academics despite their best efforts. Whatever underlies this situation, it normally creates great frustration. When adolescents experience constant failure in school and lack hope for the future, they may entertain thoughts of self-destruction.

ENVIRONMENTAL Some adolescents have incredibly sad home lives. For instance, they may be physically or sexually abused, or they may be on the front lines of nasty divorce battles. Numerous possible environmental factors can create depression. When the environmental factors become overwhelming, the youngster may decide that life is no longer worth living.

INTELLECTUAL See *Academic*.

LINGUISTIC Nearly all human activity involves language. A student with severe problems in communication or comprehension can experience tremendous insecurity and anxiety. If these feelings become overwhelming, the student may believe that she wants to end her life.

MEDICAL Some students with serious medical conditions may feel that they have been dealt bad hands in life. A student with a physical impairment can feel that she is very different from others. If the student does not accept her differences, she is vulnerable to depression, which can give rise to suicidal ideation.

PSYCHOLOGICAL Like adults, adolescents can be seriously depressed. When depression strikes, for whatever reason, there can be a sense of learned helplessness. This feeling that life will never get better and that things are hopeless can make a student think that things might be better for everyone involved if she were dead.

SOCIAL Some adolescents, for whatever reason, are never accepted by peers. Social rejections can be very stressful for some students, especially if they try hard to fit in. When this situation gets worse or persists, the student may think that she will never have any friends and will always be alone. Romantic rejections are particularly rough in this age group. Such beliefs can lead to suicidal ideation.

What to Do

If a student threatens to harm herself, we strongly recommend that you immediately consult with the school psychologist and/or the principal for reasons concerning the student's safety, your liability, the school's liability, and the parents' rights.

Tardiness

Why Students
May Exhibit This Behavior

ACADEMIC   Some students may come to school late because they have not completed their homework (possibly because they did not fully understand it) and fear the teacher's or their peers' reactions.

ENVIRONMENTAL   Chronic lateness to school often indicates a chaotic home environment with inconsistency in family routines, rules, supervision, authority, or boundaries.

INTELLECTUAL   Students with intellectual limitations may move more slowly than others, and they may be less conscious of time and less responsive to routines.

MEDICAL   Certain types of medical problems—including irritable bowel syndrome, sleep deprivation, nervous stomach, asthma—can interfere with punctuality.

PERCEPTUAL   Some students with perceptual difficulties are unable to tell time. This leads them to be late simply because they lack time information.

PSYCHOLOGICAL   In some students, depression can be a reason for chronic lateness. Pervasive depression can immobilize a student and make getting out of bed very difficult. Other students resist getting up and dawdle to act out feelings of anger and frustration that they cannot express verbally. These may be students who tend to break rules and defy authority.

SOCIAL   Some adolescents may be late to school in attempts to avoid uncomfortable confrontations. Arguments, bullying, or fear of retaliation can be at the root of chronic lateness. Other adolescents may be late to school because their friends are late and they do not want to set themselves apart.

What to Do

- Try to determine the reason for chronic lateness by asking the student. If he has shown a pattern of excessive lateness and offers a simple, illogical answer, then the truth may lie elsewhere.

- Ask the school nurse if the student has some medical condition that could cause chronic tardiness. (If this is the case, some documentation should be on file in the nurse's office.)

- Ask the school psychologist whether there are any underlying circumstances causing the student to be chronically late.

- If the student's tardiness appears related to parental issues, consider meeting or having an administrator meet with the parents to discuss the school's concerns.

- If the student's lateness appears to be rooted in his own behavior, try the following techniques:

    1. Give the student a specific responsibility to fulfill first thing in the morning to encourage punctuality.

    2. Establish consequences for lateness. For instance, if the student does not produce an acceptable excuse for being late, make him responsible for the time missed by deducting time from recess or some other recreational activity.

    3. Give the student leadership of some group activity that occurs in the morning.

    4. Praise the student for on-time arrival.

    5. Develop a behavioral contract outlining expected and acceptable behaviors along with consequences and rewards. (Your school psychologist can assist you if necessary.)

- If you have met with the parents and the student persists in being late, consult with the school counseling or social work staff, the school psychologist, or the pupil personnel team.

Teasing

Why Students
May Exhibit This Behavior

ACADEMIC   Students who feel academically inadequate may displace their inadequacy on others whom they perceive as more competent by teasing and picking on them. This behavior takes the spotlight off their academic limitations.

ENVIRONMENTAL   To a degree, teasing is part of everyday life. However, when an adolescent teases frequently or with a constant need to upset others, then the motivation may be problematic. If teasing is frequent and intense, the adolescent may well be venting some tension, frustration, or anger. Parents who tease at the expense of someone's self-esteem or pick on an adolescent to vent their own frustration can contribute to this. Also, when older siblings indulge in intense teasing of a younger student, this student in turn seeks out her own victim.

INTELLECTUAL   Students with limited intellectual ability may lack the social skills and maturity to understand fully the consequences of their teasing behavior.

LINGUISTIC   See *Perceptual*.

PERCEPTUAL   Students with perceptual deficits may not always capture the social nuances or have the social skills to monitor feedback from peers. They may tease innocently, in attempts to be funny or liked, without realizing that what they say may negatively affect others.

PSYCHOLOGICAL   Frequent and intense teasing is usually an outlet for suppressed anger or frustration. Although a student may sometimes tease the individual with whom she is angry, she may also displace her anger through teasing directed at others.

SOCIAL   Some students may tease others to gain the social spotlight and look more important in the eyes of their peers. Others may tease to elicit attention from particular individuals.

However, the teasing—depending on its extent and nature—may provoke rejection, increasing the student's social anxiety.

What to Do

- Speak with the student privately. Let her know that inappropriate teasing will not be tolerated in your classroom. Review the class rules and remind her that she must respect others.

- Speak to the class about considering other people's feelings and treating everyone with kindness.

- Remove the student from group activities when she teases inappropriately. Act immediately so that she understands that the behavior is unacceptable and she is being reprimanded for it.

- Have the student engage in self-esteem building activities.

- Consult with the school counseling or social work staff, the school psychologist, or, if necessary, the pupil personnel team.

Test Failure

Why Students
May Exhibit This Behavior

ACADEMIC   The most common reasons for failing tests involve either lack of understanding of the concepts or inadequate study skills.

ENVIRONMENTAL   Adolescents from dysfunctional or chaotic homes may not have appropriate places or sufficient quiet to study. Others may be overwhelmed with family responsibilities such as baby-sitting younger siblings.

INTELLECTUAL   Students with limited intellectual ability may simply give up if test items are too difficult for them.

LINGUISTIC   Students with language processing problems may have great difficulty understanding directions, interpreting questions, or organizing and writing essay responses.

MEDICAL   Students who miss a great deal of school because of medical problems may be unprepared for tests.

PERCEPTUAL   See *Linguistic*.

PSYCHOLOGICAL   Some students who are angry at their parents may use academic failure as a means of revenge, especially if those parents place a high value on academics. Other students who are oppositional may fail tests to send a message that they can do whatever they want, regardless of the consequences.

SOCIAL   Social preoccupation may interfere with a student's motivation or cut into study time. For some students, academic status may be incompatible with the "rules" of the social groups to which they aspire, and their lack of achievement may result from conscious decisions motivated by need for acceptance. Other students may have trouble striking an appropriate balance between academics and social involvement.

What to Do

- Review the student's records, including past teacher comments, for similar symptoms exhibited in earlier grades. Talk with the student's previous teachers about strategies that worked for them.

- Review past report cards, looking for consistent difficulties in certain subject areas.

- Review the student's group achievement test scores, which may give you some idea of skill levels. However, be aware that a student with serious learning problems may not have taken a group-administered test seriously.

- If possible, review the student's IQ scores. If you believe that the student is working up to capacity, has an average or better IQ, and yet is still failing in school, the situation warrants immediate attention.

- Meet with the school psychologist to discuss all possible reasons for the student's tendency to fail tests.

- Ask the school nurse about medical conditions that might be contributing to test failure, including hearing or vision problems and use of medications.

- Refer this student to the school counseling or social work staff or the pupil personnel team, especially if your review of the student's records has revealed a pattern of failure.

Tuning Out

Why Students
May Exhibit This Behavior

ACADEMIC   Some students will do what is required of them regardless of their interest level. Many students, however, have great difficulty attending to tasks that they find boring and may tune out for that reason. Also, students who are academically overwhelmed or confused may tune out because staying focused only reinforces their feelings of inadequacy.

ENVIRONMENTAL   For some adolescents, tuning out is related to problems at home, ranging from simple household disorganization to a nasty divorce battle or even neglect or abuse. To avoid dealing with the pain of family difficulties, these adolescents simply tune it all out. They then generalize this ability from home life to all areas of life.

INTELLECTUAL   Students with limited intelligence may lack the intellectual stamina to remain focused, especially on abstract concepts. They tend to get overwhelmed quickly and tune out. On the other hand, students with very high intelligence may tune out because they rapidly become bored in a classroom designed for average students.

LINGUISTIC   When students have difficulty understanding the language of instruction, they can become frustrated and eventually give up, tuning out what is going on around them.

MEDICAL   A student who tunes out may have a short attention span and an inability to stay on task, possibly associated with attention deficit/hyperactivity disorder (AD/HD). Students with hearing impairments may tune out because they cannot fully understand what is going on. Some students may be taking medications that create difficulties with concentration and focus.

PERCEPTUAL   Students with memory or retrieval problems may tune out when they become unable to keep up with the lessons or lectures.

PSYCHOLOGICAL   Depression and anxiety can cause some adolescents to tune out certain things. If they are worried or scared about circumstances in their lives, they will not have the mental strength to tune into what everyone else is doing.

SOCIAL   Some students tune out to academic concerns because they are preoccupied with their social lives.

What to Do

- Ask the school nurse and/or the student's parents whether the student has some medical problem underlying the tendency to tune out.

- Reduce the amount of auditory and visual stimuli in the classroom so that the student does not have too many things to focus on at one time.

- Speak privately with the student. Ask why he feels that he tunes out.

- Reinforce the student with verbal praise when you notice him on task, however briefly.

- Involve yourself with the student's activities when he needs to stay on task. Your interaction may decrease the chances of her tuning out.

- Have the student work in groups with classmates who you know have very good attention spans.

- Have the student write down exactly what he must do. Often, students who tune out have forgotten what they were required to do. Having the directions written down enables the student to get back on track.

- Try to change the topics in the classroom as often as possible. Find out how other teachers have handled this situation.

- Seat the student in the front of the class to minimize his chances of being distracted by extraneous stimuli.

- Call on the student more often than on others without making it too obvious. Keeping the student on his toes may decrease the chances that he will tune out.

- If the problem is severe and persists, consult with the school counseling or social work staff, the school psychologist, or the pupil personnel team.

Twitches or Tics

Why Students
May Exhibit This Behavior

ACADEMIC   Severe academic pressure may cause a student to release nervous tension through behavioral outlets. Twitches, tics, eye blinking, and head turning may all be forms of tension release.

ENVIRONMENTAL   If not medically based, twitches and tics may be associated with high stress levels or excessively high expectations at home.

INTELLECTUAL   Students with limited intellectual ability who regularly find themselves in situations where they are overwhelmed may exhibit twitches and tics.

LINGUISTIC   See *Academic*.

MEDICAL   Tics or twitches may be indicative of Tourette's syndrome, a neurological disorder that appears to be genetically transmitted in most cases. Tourette's is one of a number of conditions classified as tic disorders. Tics are involuntary movements that present themselves through motion or sound. The first tics or symptoms of Tourette's syndrome are usually simple motor tics of the head, face, and neck area.

- Simple motor tics are usually rapid, apparently purposeless and repetitive movements of one muscle group. Examples include eye blinking, shoulder shrugs, mouth opening, arm extending, facial grimaces, lip-licking, eye rolling, and squinting.

- Complex motor tics are involuntary movements that involve the coordinated sequence or activation of two or more muscle groups. Examples include pulling at clothes, touching people, touching objects, smelling fingers, jumping or skipping, poking or jabbing, punching, kicking, hopping, kissing oneself or others, flapping one's arms, twirling around, making thrusting movements of the groin or torso, walking on one's toes, copropraxia (sexual touching of oneself or others, obscene gestures), and self-injurious behavior.

PSYCHOLOGICAL   It is not unusual for some adolescents to vent their tensions through certain types of repetitive behaviors, such as twitching or blinking. Adolescents who are under tremendous stress may exhibit these symptoms as well. However, the frequency, intensity, and duration of the symptoms may indicate that medical causes should be considered.

SOCIAL   Extreme social stress, social confusion or worry, and so on may be vented in behavioral patterns. Adolescents who are constant victims of certain social groups or individuals may exhibit such patterns as well.

What to Do

When a student exhibits tics or twitches, we strongly recommend that you immediately consult with the school psychologist, the school nurse, and the principal for reasons concerning the student's safety, your liability, the school's liability, and the parents' rights.

Being Victimized

Why Students
May Exhibit This Behavior

ACADEMIC   Students may be victimized by peers for being either too smart or not smart enough. The school bullies may pick on academically capable students because they are excelling where the bullies are not. On the other hand, students who are not doing well academically may get picked on because of their failures.

ENVIRONMENTAL   In some homes, adolescents are taught not to fight back but rather to be passive observers. They may believe that standing up for oneself is equivalent to fighting and be afraid of possible consequences at home. Adolescents who don't stand up for themselves may be targets for bullies. Also, adolescents who are victimized at home sometimes reproduce this behavior in school. Abuse or neglect at home leads them to become fearful and compliant in order to survive. The pattern of abuse is then repeated in school by certain students who "feed off" these victims.

INTELLECTUAL   Fragile or intellectually limited students may be the victims of others because their verbal or social behaviors may be misunderstood. See also *Academic*.

LINGUISTIC   Students who have difficulties with language may have accents or speak indistinctly. Class bullies find these differences amusing and pick on these students. If they do not defend themselves, the victimization may continue for long periods.

MEDICAL   Some students may be victimized by bullies because they are medically frail or smaller than others. Their disadvantages in height and weight make them easy targets for those who look to victimize.

PSYCHOLOGICAL   Adolescents with weak egos and low self-esteem may believe that they cannot stand up for themselves on any issues. They believe themselves inferior to others. Bullies recognize this mental weakness and target them. If these adolescents do not stand up for themselves because psychologically they have given up, the bullying will most likely continue.

Certain types of characteristics, such as a fragile appearance or physical differences, may bring on victimization by other insecure students who seek to reduce their own feelings of inadequacy. These bullies have a type of "radar" that can zero in on students who will provide little resistance. The victims may be loners, nonassertive students with low self-esteem, or new students who have not yet connected to social groups.

Social   Some adolescents cannot find acceptance with peers despite their best efforts. When bullies see someone who is not fitting in socially, they may target that person, who has no friends to turn to for help. This isolation can create great anxiety and fear, often leading to increased social withdrawal.

What to Do

- Speak to the class about treating people with kindness and compassion. Make clear that you will not tolerate rude, insensitive behavior in your classroom. Establish consequences for such behavior.

- Speak privately with the student who is the target of the behavior. Ask why she feels he is always being victimized.

- Have the student work in small groups with classmates. Assign her to be group leader. Her confidence may increase dramatically because she now must be the one in charge rather than the victim.

- Invite the school counselor, the school social worker, or another mental health professional to speak to the class about respect and feelings. Hearing important information from others can be highly beneficial to a class. It can also enlighten the student being victimized about the kind of treatment she should expect from others.

- Set aside time with the student to role-play actual situations from her life. This may help her develop better coping skills.

- Consult with the school counseling or social work staff or the school psychologist about the possibility of counseling to help promote the student's self-esteem and confidence.
- Contact the parents if you believe that the student may be in danger.
- If the problem is severe and persists, consult with the school's pupil personnel team.

About the Authors

Dr. Roger Pierangelo is a New York State licensed clinical psychologist. He has years of experience as a regular classroom teacher, school psychologist, and administrator of psychology programs. He has served as full professor in the graduate Special Education Department at Long Island University; member of various committees on special education; evaluator for the New York State Education Department; director of a private clinic; and consultant to numerous private and public schools, PTAs, and SEPTA groups.

Dr. Pierangelo earned his B.S. from St. John's University, M.S. and professional diploma from Queens College, and Ph.D. from Yeshiva University. He is a member of the American Psychological Association, New York State Psychological Association, Nassau County Psychological Association, New York State Union of Teachers, and Phi Delta Kappa.

Dr. Pierangelo is the author of numerous books, including *The Survival Kit for the Special Education Teacher* and *The Special Education Teacher's Book of Lists* (Simon and Schuster), and *301 Ways to Be a Loving Parent* and *The World's Most Provocative Questions* (SPI Publishers). He is coauthor of *The Parent's Guide to Special Education, The Complete Guide to Transition Services,* and *The Special Educator's Complete Guide to 109 Diagnostic Tests* (Simon and Schuster); *The Special Education Yellow Pages* (Merrill); *Assessment in Special Education* (Allyn and Bacon); the *Pocket Therapist Series* (Adams Media); and *Why Your Students Do What They Do and What to Do When They Do It (Grades K–5)* and *What Every Teacher Should Know about Students with Special Needs* (Research Press).

Dr. George A. Giuliani is a full-time assistant professor of psychology at St. Joseph's College in Patchogue, New York. He is a New York State licensed clinical psychologist and a member of the New York Association of School Psychologists and the National Association of School Psychologists.

Dr. Giuliani earned his B.A. from the College of the Holy Cross, M.S. from St. John's University, J.D. from City University

Law School, and Psy.D. from The Graduate School of Applied and Professional Psychology at Rutgers University.

Dr. Giuliani is coauthor of *The Special Educator's Complete Guide to 109 Diagnostic Tests* (Simon and Schuster); *Assessment in Special Education* (Allyn and Bacon); the *Pocket Therapist Series* (Adams Media); and *Why Your Students Do What They Do and What to Do When They Do It (Grades K–5)* and *What Every Teacher Should Know about Students with Special Needs* (Research Press).